Democratic Citizenship and Public Administration

Democratic Dilemmas and Policy Responsiveness

Series Editors: Thomas A. Bryer and Egle Butkeviciene

Public policy issues divide societies around the world, with resulting tensions that threaten the fabric of social cohesion and certain norms of empathy, compassion, and civility. Today, such hot button issues as poverty, refugee integration, immigration, and others are the source for implicit and explicit debate concerning the "fitness" and "worthiness" of some individuals and groups of individuals to be one with society. In social and democratic terms, some citizens are included-in and some are included-out. This series consists of books that address the democratic dilemmas that arise with desire to be responsive through policy to competing values, interests, and positions. Special attention will be given to local governance, where divisions often manifest most clearly, but works that address higher levels of government, as well as supranational governments, will also be included in the series. Accepted titles will be sole- or co-authored monographs or edited volumes, with emphasis on deep case analysis, comparative case studies, comparative empirical studies, or theoretical explorations.

Recent Titles

Democratic Citizenship and Public Administration: Democratic Arrangements and Democratic Practices, by Ray C. Minor

Citizenship and Ethics: from the Neighborhood to the City, Country to the World, edited by Thomas A. Bryer and So HeeJeon

Getting Heard but Not Listened To: An Analysis of Public Participation in Environmental Impact Assessment (EIA) in Brazil, by Christiane Bená Dias

Poor Participation: Fighting the Wars on Poverty and Impoverished Citizenship, by Thomas A. Bryer and Sofia Prysmakova-Rivera

Democratic Citizenship and Public Administration

Democratic Arrangements and Democratic Practices

Ray C. Minor

LEXINGTON BOOKS
Lanham • Boulder • New York • London

Published by Lexington Books
An imprint of The Rowman & Littlefield Publishing Group, Inc.
4501 Forbes Boulevard, Suite 200, Lanham, Maryland 20706
www.rowman.com

6 Tinworth Street, London SE11 5AL, United Kingdom

British Library Cataloguing in Publication Information Available

Library of Congress Control Number: 2020952030

ISBN 978-1-7936-1748-4 (cloth : alk. paper)
ISBN 978-1-7936-1749-1 (electronic)

Contents

List of Figures and Tables

FIGURE

TABLES

Acknowledgments

I am grateful to the researchers who diligently prepared the eight reports reviewed in this book: namely, Brandi Blessett, Marijoan Bull, Larkin Dudley, Kathryn Webb-Farley, Tia Sheree Gaynor, Noel Gniady-Banford, Ellen M. Knutson, Matt Leighninger, Kara Lindaman, Hannah Tsadik, and Jacky Zvulun. Without their good works, I would have been less motivated to write this book. Thanks to the Academy for having a wealth of scholars in the field of Public Administration. Especially, thanks to Thomas Bryer, Brian Cook, Larkin Dudley, Kathryn Webb-Farley, Patricia Ripoll, and Brian Williams for making critical editorial and content suggestions on an early draft. Thanks to John Dedrick and David Mathews at the Kettering Foundation for support of this project. Thanks to Saravia Williams for graphic assistance. Thanks to Ilse Tebbetts for editing four chapters. Thanks to Laura Carlson for editing a chapter. A special thanks to Lisa Boone-Berry for editing the entire book. All errors and omissions are truly my own.

Chapter 1

Introduction

The primary purposes of this book are to provide basic understanding of democratic citizenship and to glean insights from several recent public administration reports that could be helpful in understanding the degree to which ordinary citizens were taking control of their future in the American republic. My intent was to provide theoretical and evidence-based perspectives on the complexities of citizenship in a capitalistic-republican state and its effects on persons residing within its domain. It is my hope that this book will stimulate learning for those who desire a better understanding of how democracy works and what is required for democracy to work. The book is an attempt at providing a basic understanding of public administration theory and practice. This book is unique in that it places citizenship in rich context and proposes two new theoretical frameworks for reparation and citizenship.

In large part, the approach to meeting the core objectives of this book was to illustrate, through examples, how citizens engage with government and other institutions or not. I start by offering some terminology and insights as lenses for viewing this material.

In public administration, scholars study, among other things, the *policy-making process*. So, it may be helpful to note here what that process entails. There are five stages of policy formation. The first stage is *agenda setting*. Its aim is to gain a place on the agenda and to attract the attention of policymakers. The next step is *formulation*, the preparation of alternative courses of action for dealing with public problems. *Policy decisions*, the third stage, concerns which of those choices should be adopted as policy. The next stage, *policy implementation*, involves applying a policy to its targeted population. Finally, *policy evaluation* focuses on determining the effects of those policies when put in practice (Anderson 2006, 312–317).

Citizens, on the other hand, often operate less formally. Citizens may first discuss a problem with a neighbor or two before calling a meeting (if necessary). If these citizens decide to act, they might meet more often—or at least as often as required to solve the problem. If they find that solutions are beyond their capabilities, they are likely to turn to outside resources, especially government and the private sector, to tackle the problem.

Public policy is what governments do or do not do (Shafritz and Russell 2005, 35). Held (2006) views *democracy* as "a form of government in which . . . the people rule. . . . Democracy entails a political community in which there is some form of political equality among people" (Held 2006, 1). What do citizens offer as coproducers of public goods and services? *Citizen capacity* refers to the collective resources citizens generate and possess to sustain their general welfare, especially to solve public problems. Citizens have the capacity to advance their interests and to safeguard themselves and their communities against all but major public problems. Further, citizens have the capacity to build their communities.

Citizens have limited capacities individually, but together their capacity can become enormous. It can make a difference between community and chaos, life and death, or freedom and oppression. Citizens often use their skills and resources in times of crisis. For example, they may help one another in the aftermath of a catastrophe by clearing away debris; aiding and comforting; and providing food, clothing, and shelter. In a more common example, citizens provide support for or opposition to a state referendum. They may campaign door to door, pass out leaflets and flyers, and plant yard signs.

Citizens rarely if ever attempt to solve major public problems alone. If a dam breaks and floods the community, they obviously will not attempt to solve this problem by themselves. Less disastrously, when citizens are confronted by a NIMBY problem—the proposed location of a power substation in their neighborhood, for example—individuals will recognize their limitations and seek help.

Routinely, citizens engage in public life by participating in neighborhood watch programs; property owner associations; tenant rights groups; garden clubs; book clubs; anti-crime, violence, and drug prevention task forces; sporting and recreation clubs; elections; voting leagues; deliberative forums; deliberative polls; juries; political parties; advocacy groups; social and fraternal organizations; federated organizations; religious groups; and many other voluntary associations. Citizens also participate in public meetings and hearings, register public comments, write letters to their representatives in Congress, make appeals for redress, or litigate. Citizens act collectively through democratic arrangements such as nations, states, communities, and institutions; they exercise their rights and privileges through democratic practices. These associations and practices build political and social capital and have the potential to produce social change.

Ideally—as envisioned by the founders of this nation—the role of a *democratic citizen* is to be civically literate, politically active, and protective of democratic values. Citizens exercise their First Amendment rights and their universal human rights. They organize for their collective well-being and hold their public officials accountable. They behave in ways that ensure equality for all. These democratic actions flow from the rights and immunities conferred on them by advanced democratic societies.

When public administrators speak of *citizen participation*, generally they mean allowing citizens to represent their interests and provide input at a particular level of the policymaking process. In an ideal democracy, "self-rule" is the underlying assumption. In the American context, this notion plays out in the assumption that ordinary citizens have a sense of political efficacy approximate to "self-rule." A state-centered view of politics leaves citizens little to do but inform themselves and vote (Levine 2013, 21). Even in a state-centered political environment citizens may exercise an assortment of democratic practices, such as those noted above. Unless these activities are encouraged and valued, however, the efforts of citizens working collectively outside of institutions may be insufficient, futile, or negligible. So, the big question is: What value do citizens present in public problem-solving? One answer is that citizens can become coproducers.

Elinor Ostrom (1996) defines *coproduction* to mean the process through which individuals outside of the organization contribute something of value in producing goods or services of consequence (Ostrom 1996, 1073). Therefore, when citizens and government officials are working together, that has the potential for producing synergy (Ostrom 1996, 1080). Ostrom also advanced the notion of *polycentricity in government*—an idea adopted from Vincent Ostrom, implying many centers of decision-making independent of each other (2012, 15).

If public administrators would work on public problems side by side with citizens or in association with citizens (coproduction) these efforts would make for a stronger democracy. A better alignment with democratic practices would go far in ameliorating the anger and distrust many citizens feel for governmental and nongovernmental institutions, by strengthening democratic self-rule.

Today's citizens not only do have little confidence in institutions but, in dealing with the problems and issues on their agendas, many of those same institutions see few roles to be played by citizens. Birkland (2005) defines *institutions* as organizations and systems with which individuals interact and achieve political and policy goals through rules and policy procedures (Birkland 2005, 52). In an ideal situation, ordinary citizens would have a primary role in naming and framing the problems and issues that require policymaking—that is, defining them in terms that are relevant to them in their everyday lives. In all too many cases, these issues are named and framed by experts and professionals in ways that have little if any relationship to the way they affect citizens or the things citizens care most about.

Generally, when citizens act publicly it is about something they care about or that troubles them—something they want to participate in, control, correct, or resolve. The most challenging issues for citizens to deal with are those that have been termed "wicked problems." These are multidimensional problems tangled to such an extent that ameliorative efforts often compound rather than cure them. This notion originated with Rittel and Webber (1973) who considered many planning problems and social problems in general akin to being malignant as opposed to benign (Rittel and Webber 1973, 160).

Amitai Etzioni (1996) defines *community* as a web of affect-laden relationships among a group of individuals; a set of shared values, norms, and meanings; history and identity; and a relatively high level of responsiveness (Etzioni 1996, 5). I would add that community is not monolithic but rather stratified along racial, ethnic, cultural, political, social, religious, and economic lines.

In regard to the remaining text, chapter 2 presents a literature review on citizen participation. This chapter provides a background for understanding the nuanced ways institutional designs were applied to engaging "affected citizens" and "stakeholders." This chapter reveals that there is no one right way for public participation nor is there consensus for doing so.

In chapter 3, I delve more deeply into the political theory and practice of public administration. Concepts relating to public administration, citizen participation and engagement, and special interest groups are discussed. This chapter adds depth to understanding the boundaries of public participation in representative government.

Under joint learning agreements with the Kettering Foundation, researchers explored coproduction or complementary acting between citizens and institutions. A part of Kettering's research portfolio focuses on citizens working with institutions. In this series of reports immediately following in chapter 4, all but the New Zealand study was under contract with the foundation.

In chapter 4, the first two research reports explore federal agencies. The initial report examines the Department of Education, the Environmental Protection Agency, the Health and Human Services Department, and the Department of Housing and Urban Development to discover coproduction of public goods and services; the second one examines the Department of Agriculture, the Department of Energy, the Department of Interior, the Department of Justice, the Department of Transportation, and the Department of Homeland Security with regard to their efforts to engage citizens in coproduction. A third report examines the Los Angeles Fire Department and its complementary relations with community members in delivering fire and rescue services. The fourth report explores Faith in Florida, an NGO devoted to addressing racial and economic issues that cause poverty, and its work with formerly incarcerated persons in restoring voting rights.

Another set of four reports are presented here. The first report investigates how a small town (Fairborn, Ohio) attempted to name and frame a problem and engage citizens in the process. The second report explores a Safe Routes to School initiative (West Springfield, Massachusetts) and the use of deliberative forums in collective decision-making. The third report examines another small town (Winona, Minnesota) as a case study in open and closed decision-making processes around transportation issues and the search for common ground between citizens and public officials. The last report focuses on participatory budgeting in Chicago. It investigates a case in which citizens were permitted to plan an alderman's discretionary budget.

In order to provide an international perspective, two cases were selected and documented below from New Zealand and Ethiopia. The New Zealand case explored public participation, voting methods, and the role of media in elections. In the second case, the focal point was Ethiopian elders and an NGO engaging in civil society on a small scale in a very limited public space. In total, the ten reports provided perspectives on the nature of citizen engagement with a variety of institutions.

Chapters 5 and 6 are more detailed case studies that illustrate in one case successful and in the other less successful, outcomes of efforts to engage citizens in the business of governing themselves. The first is a study of the Arlington Park neighborhood, a historic district in Birmingham, Alabama, conducted by the author in 2007. This research documents efforts of citizens to eradicate the incidence of illegal drugs and prostitution activities in their neighborhood. The second case study in chapter 6, conducted by the author in 2013, concerns the New Jersey Turnpike Authority and provides an anatomy of the most common form of public participation—public hearing.

Chapter 7, "Justice and Democratic Citizenship," explores the concept of justice and advances a theory of reparation. This chapter declares citizens as sovereign in a democratic state, and justice as that state's chief purpose. It proposes a new construct of reparation as a remedy for righting injustices perpetrated against certain classes of people, especially those of color.

Chapter 8 explores the problematic concept of citizenship in America. The chapter draws attention to salient issues associated with citizenship, advances legal citizenship status, discusses several models of citizenship, and offers a framework for a new theory of citizenship.

A conclusion is provided in chapter 9. Finally, in chapter 10, David Mathews offers some afterthoughts on loss of confidence in institutions, and how citizens could work with institutions as an approach to public problem-solving.

Chapter 2

Citizen Participation Research

INTRODUCTION

Over the last thirty-five years, empirical researchers on citizen participation in public policymaking explored various aspects of citizen involvement and employed numerous methodologies. Some researchers found a paradoxical relationship between government intentions and citizen involvement in public policy decision-making. King et al. (1998) observed that government desired citizens to be active but not "too active" (King et al. 1998, 318). Other researchers identified citizen involvement in public hearings as the most common of the numerous forms of citizen participation but not most effective (Brody et al. 2003; Cole and Caputo 1984; King et al. 1998). Kihl (1985) examined whether citizen participation in public hearings heightened public awareness and had impact on final policy decision-making. Myriad issues addressed in the studies struck at the core of democratic principles. Inherent in these principles was maintaining harmony in the administrative state while living up to the ideals of democracy.

Collectively, three salient questions emerged around the notion of citizen participation: What level of involvement should citizens have in making public policy? What mechanism should be used to generate citizen input in public policy? What effect should citizens have on the final policy decision? Those questions were addressed in the studies selected for this chapter. In total, the existing research shone new light on the interconnected, overlapping, and often conflicting findings of the citizen participation case studies.

Cole and Caputo (1984) explored whether citizen participation in public hearings

> had a substantial impact on final decisions to spend more funds on human services and fewer dollars on traditional services, such as public safety (Cole and Caputo 1984, 408). They hypothesized that citizen input would influence the outcome of expenditures and would result in a change in the norm as related to decisions about public funds allocations. They further hypothesized that citizen involvement in public hearings would have the positive impact of increasing public interest in matters of community affairs. (Cole and Caputo 1984, 408)

Cole and Caputo found that cities holding public hearings allocated more funds to social services and less to public safety than cities not holding hearings (Cole and Caputo 1984, 411). That outcome implied that participants in public hearings preferred social services over public safety and, as a result, influenced policy decisions. They also found that cities holding public hearings show greater public interest than those cities holding none (Cole and Caputo 1984, 411). Cole and Caputo found that participants' voices not only influenced local government's decision to spend more dollars on social services, but also made a difference in terms of generating greater public interest in their community's public hearing process (Cole and Caputo 1984, 411). The finding indicated that public hearings made a difference in terms of influencing decision-making and stimulating public interest.

In addition, they observed that there appears to be a relationship between public hearings and allocations to operating expenses, capital outlays, and new programs (Cole and Caputo 1984, 412). That statement suggested that public administrators may have paid attention to citizen input regarding these items or those citizens may have expressed an opinion on the proportionality of these particular items. Cole and Caputo concluded that the public hearing has little effect on government behavior (Cole and Caputo 1984, 415). That statement appeared to be inconsistent with their findings, which claimed that public hearings made a difference. Cole and Caputo meant that public hearings tended to make a difference in specific instances but not in general. That overall, the public hearing has had little lasting effect on decision or behavior (Cole and Caputo 1984, 415). Cole and Caputo concluded that the public hearing process may not be open and may permit sanctioned isolation of agencies and agency officials. Officials may be seeking as little program and policy change as possible (Cole and Caputo 1984, 415). King et al. (1998), who considered the public hearing as an ineffective mechanism for public participation, also reflected that sentiment. In the end, the public hearings were controlled by public officials from start to finish.

Kihl (1985) argued that the public hearing was a good mechanism for involving citizens in the policymaking process (Kihl 1985, 200). She explored whether citizen participation attracts a wide range of community interest (Kihl 1985, 186). Kihl hypothesized that well-managed hearings can engender broad-based citizen participation and become vehicles responsive to citizen frustration (Kihl 1985, 186). Kihl examined how a sample of highway hearings overcame barriers, reduced frustration, and furthered communication (Kihl 1985, 187). She concluded that design hearings can be important processes for achieving participation goals in state action plans (Kihl 1985, 199). Kihl established a relationship between the affected property's ownership and one's concern. However, Kihl also indicated that there was a range of levels for that concern (Kihl 1985, 190).

She found that citizen participation was affected by the type of project and the specifics associated with the project (Kihl 1985, 193). Perhaps, citizens were more attracted to projects that roused their interests and they were, therefore, more likely to participate in public hearings addressing the same. Kihl reported that officials gained credibility by admitting lack of information as opposed to evading questions (Kihl 1985, 198). In general, citizens recognized when public officials were not being straightforward and responded accordingly. She also stated that her study focused solely on hearings held at the project design stage where typically citizens have an opportunity to fine-tune the project (Kihl 1985, 199).

Intriguing though, Kihl found that 90 percent of the highway projects changed as a result of citizen involvement (Kihl 1985, 198). She stated, public hearings provide citizens the opportunity for participation (Kihl 1985, 200). King et al. (1998) did not find that kind of citizen involvement to be authentic. Dahl (1998) argued that if citizens did not have control of the agenda, they were not politically equal, a prerequisite in democratic society.

The level of citizen participation in public hearings was addressed by King et al. (1998). King et al. examined public discussions between experts, focus groups, and public administrators in northern Ohio. Seeking to answer the research question of how to "engender effective and satisfying participatory processes" (King et al. 1998, 317), King et al. found that in order to improve or increase the level of participation among citizens, changes must occur in the roles and relationships of all stakeholders. Stakeholders, in this case, included professionals offering expert testimony on proposed policy issues, citizens affected by those issues, and administrators making and implementing policy decisions.

King et al. asserted that there was a historic contradiction in the intention of government's ideal of public participation and limitation on active citizens (King et al. 1998, 318). King et al. also introduced the concept of "authentic public participation," qualifying it as "more than simply finding the right tools and techniques for increasing public involvement in public decisions" (King et al. 1998, 317). They argued that authentic public participation required a reexamination of the underlying roles of and relationships that should exist between administrators and citizens. King et al. posited that citizen participation was more than superficial involvement but was also a mechanism that provided opportunities for citizens to have meaningful influence in policymaking. For the process to be authentic and effective, the authors argued, there must be "deep and continuous involvement in administrative processes with the potential for all involved having an effect on the situation" (King et al. 1998, 320).

The notion held by King et al. was consistent with Dahl's (1998) theory on democracy. Dahl posited the need for adult citizens to have an opportunity to affect policy decisions. Dahl argued that citizens must control the agenda. King et al. concluded that an effective model of authentic participation must incorporate a three-pronged approach that would seek to (1) empower and educate all community members, (2) reteach administrators, and (3) enable administrative structures and processes.

In a case study of citizen involvement in public meetings about a proposed landfill, McComas and Scherer (1998) inquired about the peculiar issue of whether citizens participating represented those not attending the meeting. McComas and Scherer's research project had merit because those who were not present had no voice but were left to live with the situation or suffer the consequences. The citizen's plight intersected a deeper question of whether representative government was indeed representative. Citizens' interest, if different from the population represented, may not be served or protected.

In such a case, government may not have been so representative after all. A second question by McComas and Scherer explored whether public hearings in effect met the needs of those who organized the hearings rather than those who participated in the meetings. That question tugged at the heart of the ideals of democratic or elite models. The meta question was whether the process of policymaking should be controlled from top-down or bottom-up.

In a secondary analysis of survey data mailed to property owners, McComas and Scherer found that respondents who participated in public meetings were "demographically representative of respondents not attending the meetings" (McComas and Scherer 1998, 358). Populations were not monolithic, so demographic representation may not have equated to public opinion being the same for every similar population. Just because a subset of a population is extrapolated from a population does not necessarily mean that the two resulting populations would hold the same opinion about a situation or problem. Further, the composition of a population may have been altered or different from the actual opinion of a particular population.

McComas and Scherer also reported that there was a high degree of anger and worry among citizens most affected by a proposed landfill decision (McComas and Sherer 1998, 359). Not surprising, citizens with more at stake would hold stronger opinions and be more likely to participate in public hearings to express their concerns and protect their interests. The authors also found that the hearings better served the needs of the organizers.

Koontz (1999) found that citizen participation differed depending on the economic interests of citizens involved and whether the issues addressed were generated at the local or national level. Specifically, Koontz examined two questions: (a) whether participants who sought economic policy goals had more influence in agency policymaking decisions than those citizens who pursued noneconomic goals, and (b) whether citizens responded differently when participating in state policymaking as opposed to national policymaking (Koontz 1999, 449). Koontz argued there was a difference between citizens pursuing economic and noneconomic goals on national and local levels. And he suggested that participants who favored economic goals were more likely to participate in policymaking proceedings and would have greater influence in decisions that occur at the state level (Koontz 1999, 441). Perhaps, the state and local levels are where ordinary citizens have most contact with public officials.

Koontz established that both officials and participants thought that citizens who had economic interests were more likely to participate at the state level while citizens with noneconomic interests were more likely to participate at the national level (Koontz 1999, 443). He concluded that citizen participation empowers citizens by not only strengthening the link between the masses who are governed and leaders who do the governing, but also by substantially affecting policy outcomes (Koontz 1999, 449). To what extent do citizens generate enough power to effect public policy? I am not convinced that their power is sufficient or effective in most cases.

In their study of public participation, Beierle and Konisky (2000) reported that public participation played a central role in environmental management innovations. Seeking to discern critical aspects of public involvement in environmental matters, they examined three issues: (a) what could be gained from greater citizen involvement in decision-making, (b) what variables make some programs succeed and others fail, and (c) how to best introduce public values into the governmental decision-making equation in order to build trust among stakeholders (Beierle and Konisky 2000, 587). The authors hypothesized that the push for more citizen participation would lead to greater participation and "improve the substantive and procedural quality of decisions" (Beierle and Konisky 2000, 587).

Beierle and Konisky found that "when done well" citizen participation could accomplish critical social goals. A good deliberative process allowed participants to discuss and debate issues and arrive at consensus (Beierle and Konisky 2000, 596). They also discovered that a particular program's success appeared to be unrelated to the number of issues surrounding the complexity of a particular decision (Beierle and Konisky 2000, 599). Beierle and Konisky argued that citizen participation played an important role in all aspects of environmental issues (Beierle and Konisky 2000, 587). Overall findings supported an "optimistic view" of citizen participation (Beierle and Konisky 2000, 587) and suggested that public involvement could play an important role in the future of environmental management.

Beierle and Konisky noted that findings from the environmental study revealed that public administrators and citizens could have communicated more than they did. The researchers suggested the need for greater emphasis on the role of communication between public administrators and citizens.

In a study of citizen involvement in the planning process used to plan the development and expansion of the Monongahela National Forest of West Virginia, Steelman (2001) discovered that both participatory and elite forms of decision-making contributed to planning. Steelman addressed the question of whether a "participatory or elite model" (Steelman 2001, 71) best characterized the decision-making process of the public agency.

A critical historical question facing public administrators was whether to utilize a top-down or bottom-up approach. Under the administrative state of the 1930s, 1940s, and1950s, public administration was usually top-down. Steelman hypothesized that "a more participatory decision would be affiliated with success" (Steelman 2001, 72). However, she discovered that neither an elite nor a participatory model of decision-making was more dominant in the planning process. Instead both forms of decision-making aided officials in deciding important plan elements (Steelman 2001, 71).

Steelman concluded that citizen participation should play an important and specific role in policymaking and should be used like any policy tool by decision-makers with "with care and practical intent" (Steelman 2001, 86). If citizen participation were simply a policy tool, then democratic principles were rendered less meaningful. That position meant that policy decisions could be made without regard to citizen input. Steelman implied that citizen participation was optional or appropriate *if* it fitted or *when* it fitted. If it were not appropriate, then one should have left that particular policy tool in the toolbox.

Two questions surfaced from that study: (1) To whom did public officials and administrators owe their allegiance? (2) Should citizens be viewed as valuable stakeholders who were truly vested in public policy decisions? In Dahl's democratic regime, the allegiance of public officials and administrators was owed to the people. If citizens were viewed from that perspective, then there would be little questioning about their involvement in public policymaking. Technically, citizens own government in any constituted democratic form including representative government.

The government's role in mandating citizen participation was the focus of an extensive study conducted by Brody et al. (2003) that examined how citizen participation choices were incorporated into planning mandates of ten state-growth management programs. Brody et al. reported that government mandates did affect local government's attention toward citizen involvement in the state of New Jersey, as well as Florida, Georgia, Hawaii, Maine, Maryland, Oregon, Rhode Island, Vermont, and Washington.

Seeking to understand the common connection, Brody et al. investigated the degree to which citizen involvement mandates and other planning practices resulted in broader citizen participation in the planning process (Brody et al. 2003, 245). They hypothesized that mandates employed by local governments would create broader citizen participation (Brody et al. 2003, 245). They reasoned that citizen's lack of interest in being active participants in the planning process could be overcome if officials were able to "craft lively and engaging participation programs" (Brody et al. 2003, 260). Findings showed that the mandates did have an effect on local government's "attention to citizen involvement" (Brody et al. 2003, 260) and did, in fact, affect the choices planners made in developing citizen participation programs.

The mandates also had an effect on the level of public participation (Brody et al. 2003, 260), according to Brody et al. They identified six factors that planners must consider in designing participation programs:

(1) whether to prepare and staff a participation plan;
(2) whether to educate citizens, seek their preferences, or grant influence;
(3) whether to involve them in the process;
(4) which type of stakeholders group to involve;
(5) what types of participation methods; and
(6) what types of information and dissemination process to incorporate (Brody et al. 2003, 246).

Brody et al. concluded that if city planners were "serious" about increasing and strengthening citizen involvement, then they should be open to revising outdated requirements regarding citizens (Brody et al. 2003, 261). They found that most state-growth management laws were vague, outdated, and provided little guidance for planners (Brody et al. 2003, 246). The questioning of commitment to citizen participation by Brody et al. implied that they perceived overall there was not effective or authentic citizen participation in plan making in the ten cases studied.

Brody et al. hypothesized that government mandates of citizen involvement in local planning increased broader participation. Even so, the power of agenda setting and policy formation were still left in the hands of public officials, administrators, and experts.

In examining the effects of "quality citizen participation" in the United States Forest Service (USFS) planning process, Halvorsen (2003, 540) explored whether quality public participation could have a positive and transformative effect on the beliefs of participants. She hypothesized that "high-quality" public involvement could be a first step in resolving issues of trust between USFS and citizens (Halvorsen 2003, 535). She defined high-quality participation as satisfying, accessible, and deliberative (Halvorsen 2003, 536). She found that exposure to comfortable and convenient meetings was strongly associated with positive expectations of performance (Halvorsen 2003, 541).

Halvorsen argued the findings suggested that quality participation may have both long- and short-term effects on citizens who participated (Halvorsen 2003, 541). On the other hand, she argued that multiple exposures to quality participation could lead to significant changes in the beliefs of participants (Halvorsen 2003, 541). She maintained that the overall findings showed there were some specific aspects of "quality participation" that were positive expectations regarding the agency's responsiveness and performance (Halvorsen 2003, 535). According to Dahl (1998), the goal would be to enlighten citizens' discretion and not manipulate them. Nevertheless, Halvorsen's research on quality public participation sought to understand the effects of short- and long-term effects on participants. In republican governance, the role of government should not be to steer citizens into the government's plan but to be influenced by what citizens suggest the plan should be.

In a 2004 study on public meetings, Adams reported that such meetings offered venues for citizens to achieve their political goals while simultaneously increasing government accountability and responsiveness. His research question explored the role citizen participation played in public policymaking. Do public meetings have a role to play in fostering citizen participation in policymaking (Adams 2004, 43)?

Adams asserted that public meetings were important to the democratic process and allowed citizens the opportunity to share valuable information with local leaders (Adams 2004, 43). More specific, Adams posited that there were six benefits to public meetings:

(1) they could be an effective way to convey information about public opinion to officials (Adams 2004, 46);
(2) they provided opportunities to citizens for supporting friendly elected officials who take controversial policy stands and for expressing displeasure with officials with whom they disagree (Adams 2004, 47);
(3) they offered citizens opportunities to vent, criticize, or offer support to the proposed policy (Adams 2004, 48);
(4) they allowed citizens to influence the agenda (Adams 2004, 49);
(5) they were an excellent venue for asking for a delay (Adams 2004, 50); and

(6) they provided a forum where citizens can communicate with each other (Adams 2004, 50).

He concluded that meetings that utilized citizen participation had the important role of serving as the venue in which citizen participation could "achieve their political goals" (Adams 2004, 43).

Adams was among the few scholars who found multiple reasons for why public meetings added value to public decision-making. However, what appeared to elude Adams was that citizens did not exercise effective or authentic participation, as defined by Dahl (1998) and King et al. (1998). There were three implications from Adams's research. First, there was value in public meetings even if they did or did not influence policy decisions; second, citizens had a public venue for venting their opinions and criticizing policy proposals; and third, citizens had opportunity to communicate with one another.

In a study to discern appropriate public participation processes, Webler and Tuler (2006) concluded that a good process reached out to all stakeholders, shared information, engaged people, and satisfied multiple interests. Webler and Tuler sought to examine what was the most "appropriate" (Webler and Tuler 2006, 699) public participation process for matters related to environmental assessment and decision-making (Webler and Tuler 2006, 699).

Webler and Tuler hypothesized that having an understanding of how citizens want to participate and what they want to gain from the process are critical to creating a "legitimate and effective process" that is meaningful to all stakeholders (Webler and Tuler 2006, 700). They found that across the ten case studies investigated, there were limited agreement and differences of opinions on the qualities of a good process (Webler and Tuler 2006, 699). Webler and Tuler's findings below were consistent with Dahl's (1998) notion of effective participation and also supported what King et al. (1998) called "authentic participation." They found that the results of their study challenged officials to consider the importance of the "diversity of participants" and the need to have representative perspectives when developing public participation processes (Webler and Tuler 2006, 699).

Webler and Tuler also found that there were "clearly distinct perspectives" (Webler and Tuler 2006, 718) for defining what was appropriate for the public participation process. Hence, they identified four perspectives:

(1) science-centered stakeholder consultation;
(2) egalitarian deliberation;
(3) efficient cooperation; and
(4) informed collaboration (Weber and Tuler 2006, 718).

Those factors provided representations of participants' preferences for processes defined by the conditions of instruction (Webler and Tuler 2006, 710).

Hamlett and Cobb (2006), in a study of group deliberation as related to the risks and benefits of nanotechnology, found that there was little evidence in support of the concept of "polarization cascade" (Hamlett and Cobb 2006, 631). In other words, there were minimum traces of majority influence over minority opinion in a group's deliberative setting. Hamlett and Cobb postulated that polarization cascades occurred when "individuals holding the minority opinion in a group adopt the majority opinion after deliberating" (Hamlett and Cobb 2006, 631).

To address that issue, researchers explored the hypothesis that group deliberation was often "biased toward the original majority preferences because of cognitive and affective errors in decision making" (Hamlett and Cobb 2006, 629). The primary research question was "whether after deliberating the mean opinion within a group moves in the direction initially favored by a majority" (Hamlett and Cobb 2006, 635). In other words, did the majority opinion dominate after a period of deliberation?

A secondary question examined whether it was possible to create deliberative environments that would "meet deliberative democracy proponents' expectations while simultaneously avoiding polarization cascades" (Hamlett and Cobb 2006, 632). The researchers utilized two focus groups and examined two key variables: "task facilitation" and "quality of the argument pool" (Hamlett and Cobb 2006, 629) to answer those questions. They also measured another set of dependent variables related to participants' priority rankings of the risks benefits of nanotechnology (Hamlett and Cobb 2006, 635). The authors measured participants' subjective opinions about nanotechnology because the literature identified those variables as being affected by polarization cascades (Hamlett and Cobb 2006, 645).

Hamlett and Cobb found "limited evidence" in support of polarization cascades, particularly as "not replicated for any particular measure of participant's opinions" (Hamlett and Cobb 2006, 636). In their opinion, evidence supporting the existence of polarization cascades was "minimal" (Hamlett and Cobb 2006, 643). They concluded that "deliberations . . . structured to mitigate or possibly avoid polarization cascades . . . can only be tentative and suggestive" (Hamlett and Cobb 2006, 643). Careful attention must be paid in conducting deliberations to avoid polarization cascades.

In a study of citizen participation in an FCC ownership proceeding, McGregor (2006) sought to determine the utility or viability of public comments on commissioners' policy decisions. He reported that public comments did not present the specific information that the commission used to justify its expert opinions. The broader question of the study was "whether e-mail comments contained the kind of written feedback that could be considered necessary for meaningful public participation" (McGregor 2006, 207). McGregor conducted a content analysis of the FCC's records to examine whether comments made by citizens from their individual e-mail comments provided specific information that was both "relevant" and "timely" (McGregor 2006, 209).

McGregor hypothesized that if citizens wanted to have a role in setting rules then they needed to have specific substantive knowledge about the proceedings (McGregor 2006, 209). A second hypothesis was that e-mail comments that either knowingly or unknowingly misstated facts or provided misleading or irrelevant information would not likely be considered as a part of the proceedings (McGregor 2006, 209). McGregor also sought to determine whether public participation would need to be timely in order to be accepted (McGregor 2006, 209). Findings of the study revealed that of the 1,400 e-mail comments that were reviewed, only two favored some aspect of the commission's deregulatory proposal.

McGregor reported that the loss of viewpoint diversity was the major casualty of those filing comments (McGregor 2006, 217). The two most dominant themes cited by McGregor concerned the effects of further deregulation on democratic principles and the agency ignoring the public interests in favor of corporate interests, respectively (McGregor 2006, 220). He concluded that while most of the comments addressed relevant topics in logical ways, the comments did not present the kind of "specific information that the commission uses to justify its expert opinions" (McGregor 2006, 207). This conclusion, however, begged the question of the meaningfulness of having public participation: If the goal of a public agency were to justify expert opinions, then why bother about citizen participation? Why not tell citizens that their opinions mattered only if they agreed with expert opinions? Further, why not just inform them that the public hearing process was autocratic?

McGregor argued that several factors had been identified that may have affected the relative impact of individual citizen's comments in administrative agency proceedings. He concluded that if citizens through their e-mail were to have an impact on administrative decision-making, the individual citizens who commented would have to provide the agency with timely and relevant information provided within the deadlines set by the agency.

In their national survey of city and county administrators, Yang and Callahan (2007) reported that, on average, although local governments used citizen-involvement mechanisms frequently, they were less likely to use their input into decision-making. Yang and Callahan explored four research questions: What social or political groups in the community promote citizen involvement? Which of these groups are likely to succeed? What barriers obstruct citizen involvement efforts? Do administrative attitudes make a difference (Yang and Callahan 2007, 249)? The authors hypothesized that involving citizens in administrative processes reflects administrative responsiveness (Yang and Callahan 2007, 249).

Of a survey of 932 city and county managers, 428 valid surveys were returned (Yang and Callahan 2007, 252–253). The national survey of city and county administrators was also designed to examine the theory of "bureaucratic responsiveness" (Yang and Callahan 2007, 252) regarding public participation. The study also looked at the importance of stakeholders' roles in influencing citizens and found that while local governments frequently used citizen involvement as a participatory tool, officials were less likely to use citizen input in final decision-making (Yang and Callahan 2007, 254). In other words, citizen participation mechanisms were pseudo (going through the motions) to adhere to the law and to gain public approval of administrative plans.

Yang and Callahan found that public managers who were from larger communities often reported positive attitudes regarding citizen participation. The authors also found public involvement mechanisms that were often selected in larger communities (Yang and Callahan 2007, 254). According to the study, city government and other governmental agencies were also perceived as being enthusiastic about promoting citizen participation efforts (Yang and Callahan 2007, 255). Survey responses from city and county administrators revealed the top five obstacles to citizen involvement in descending order:

(1) 71 percent felt that "citizens don't have time";
(2) 61 percent cited that "citizens promote their own agenda";
(3) 54 percent thought "citizens don't trust government";
(4) 53 percent indicated "inadequate government-citizen communication"; and
(5) 51 percent reported that "participation objectives [were] poorly defined" (Yang and Callahan 2007, 255).

Yang and Callahan concluded that citizen participation efforts by local governments did reflect "bureaucratic responsiveness to participating values, stakeholder pressures, and administrative practicality" (Yang and Callahan 2007, 256). Additionally, they concluded that public managers were the ones who ultimately controlled the participatory process and its outcome, deciding who would participate as well as how citizen values and concerns would be conveyed publicly and incorporated into decision-making (Yang and Callahan 2007, 256).

In reflecting on the findings and conclusions drawn by Yang and Callahan, one could infer that citizens were not politically equal as ascribed by Dahl (1998). Nor was citizen participation authentic as espoused by King et al. (1998). Yang and Callahan found that elected officials were perceived by respondents as the strongest proponents of citizen involvement (Yang and Callahan 2007, 256). That finding was not surprising since elected officials often create the appearance of caring about public opinion, especially during reelection time. Yang and Callahan concluded that public managers responded more positively to elected officials, businesses, and nonprofits because of their perceived power and legitimacy (Yang and Callahan 2007, 260). The implication was that public managers were key in determining what influencers were heard on policy matters.

In his study on public participation mechanisms, Woods (2009) stated that public participation procedures were associated with greater influence by courts, other agencies, and the governor (Woods 2009, 525). Woods explored three research questions in his study:

(1) Do mechanisms designed to promote public access lead to greater participation in agency rulemaking?
(2) If participation does increase, does this, in turn, lead to greater external influence over the content of agency rules? and
(3) Which outside institutions or groups benefit most from these mechanisms? (Woods 2009, 519).

Woods hypothesized that states would vary significantly in terms of the types of opportunities that provided for public participation, specifically related to administrative rulemaking during all stages of the "the rulemaking process" (Woods 2009, 519). To test that hypothesis, Woods sent 991 agency directors in fifteen states "a unique survey" (Woods 2009, 521) during the summer of 2000. Woods speculated that there would be "greater public notification associated with significant increases in the amount of influence agency heads report other agencies, courts, and the governor having" (Woods 2009, 523).

Additionally, he suggested that increased levels of public access would be associated with significant increases in the impact that agency officials, interest groups, other agencies, and courts would have in the process of rulemaking (Woods 2009, 523). Woods found that the mechanism of public participation was associated with increases in the influence of various factors related to agency rules (Woods 2009, 523). He also found that critics would likely understate the importance of public notifications and procedures related to access (Woods 2009, 525).

According to Woods, public participation mechanisms that provided organized interests with increased access served to increase their impact as related to administrative rules (Woods 2009, 525). Moreover, Woods found that public participation procedures were associated with greater influence by public agencies such as courts, other agencies, and the government as related to administrative decision-making (Woods 2009, 525). That finding was not surprising, as many active citizens presume such conditions to be the case. The significant implication in this study was that the governor, agencies, and the courts had greater influence on policymaking than others, including ordinary citizens. Those not included in the elite groups were relegated to second-class status.

SUMMARY

The scholars highlighted in this chapter have conceptualized and applied a variety of methods to engage "affected citizens" and "stakeholders" in the public policymaking process over time. However, even after decades of trial and error, there is no consensus on the right method or what the ideal method would look like. Further, there is little agreement on when or at what level to include the public, if at all, in public policymaking processes.

Many of the public participation methods do include democratic features but none of the ones discussed above could be classified as being effectively democratic. Therefore, citizens or community residents are pulled into myriad processes that result in their effectiveness being subject to debate. In spite of these challenges, these participatory methods do have some benefits.

Needless to say, if ordinary citizens are to make a difference in controlling their collective future, it is necessary to work with and through institutions of all kinds. The major vehicles for change are the large institutions—governmental and nongovernmental—both public and private. These institutions are the arenas where change happens. Therefore, the level of citizen participation and the effect of this participation in and on these important political arrangements determine the degree of control ordinary citizens have on their common destiny.

Based on the studies above, there are mixed findings about public participation. Beyond discussion of different models and their effectiveness, it appears that even the best intended are not quite democratic in the sense that citizens and community members design, control, and plan their resources and actions. None expressed this point of view nor were any completely democratic.

Chapter 3 delves more deeply into the political theory and practice of public administration. Concepts are discussed about public administration, citizen participation, and engagement and special-interest groups. This chapter adds depth to understanding the boundaries of public participation in representative government.

Chapter 3

Public Administration and Citizen Participation

INTRODUCTION

In order to better understand institutions and how they work with citizens and vice versa, I explored some of the political philosophy undergirding the theory and practice of public administration. Also, I hypothesized that a better understanding of how and to what extent citizens were engaging in public policy decisions might also indicate how and to what extent they were controlling their collective future. Perhaps, the best chance citizens or community members have to control their common future in advanced technological society is working with and through institutions.

In general, public administration is what governments do or do not do. I expound upon this definition below. Citizens or community members in the United States live under the auspices of government and therefore are bound by the rule of law. Given this restraint, it matters what citizens or community members do or do not do to control their collective future. Citizen participation in any form of democratic practice is the best pathway for navigating common destiny.

"PUBLIC ADMINISTRATION

As with the foundation of any field, the epistemology is evolutionary. Public administration is no different in that regard as indicated by scholars cited below. The field is interdisciplinary and therefore susceptible to academic encroachment or overlapping borders. Many scholars agree that the essence of public administration is the managing and delivering of services to the public, and that publicness separates public administration from private management.

Lan and Anders (2000, 162) found in their research on the study of public administration that the foremost guiding paradigm was publicness. Or, as Cook argued that what makes public administration and public management public and distinctive is that politics is at the heart of the enterprise (Cook 1998, 229). Further, the proper role and function of administrative agencies are intended to be driven by laws and not profit or special interests. Administrative agencies too, though some scholars may disagree, serve citizens and not customers. The essence of public administration is serving the "common good."

Across the course of American political development, the message has been that the administrative should be removed from the political (Cook 1998, 226). In his seminal paper entitled *The Study of Administration*, Wilson (1887) asserted,

> The field of administration is a field of business. It is removed from the hurry and strife of politics; it at most points stands apart even from the debatable ground of constitutional study . . . administration lies outside the proper sphere of politics. Administrative questions are not political questions. Although politics sets the tasks for administration, it should not manipulate its offices. (Wilson 1887, 28)

Wilson's assertions that administration is a field of business and that it is removed from the strife of politics are not well grounded and have long been refuted. Business is not the only organizational model, and government is not business. Government is an organizational model that is public administration. Business is private management. Public administration is the management of all things public. Politics is intertwined and inseparable from administration. People constitute public administration not so much robots and machines. In this scenario, people make decisions many of which are political in nature. Public administration is not, in its entirety, clinical meaning unemotional and detached as Wilson presumes. Public administration is as much a political institution as any legislature, court, or office of elected executive (Cook 1998, 225). This distinction appears to be settled principle. The two functions often operate in tandem. However, the two functions of government may for purposes of convenience be designated as politics and administration.

Politics is the power people exercise to influence or sway others to adapt, accept, or submit to their way. This power may operationalize on a personal, group, or mass level. Politics has to do with policies or expressions of the will of citizens, state, or special interests. Administration has to do with the execution of these policies (Goodnow1900:Shafritz, Hyde & Parkes, 2004, 35). Politics is about making decisions, influencing people, building relationships, and exercising power.

Leonard D. White (1954) argued:

> Public administration is the management of [people] and materials in the accomplishment of the purposes of the state. . . . The objective of public administration is the most efficient utilization of the resources at the disposal of officials and employees. . . . The scientific management movement has had a very important share in stimulating improvement in the methods of carrying on public business. . . . The enormous improvements which have been made by scientific management in some industries have raised the question whether or not equally striking improvements are feasible in government. (White 1954, 57–62)

In hindsight, it appears fallacious to assert that the methods and practices of one sector might have equal effects in another. Benefiting from the passing of time, we find that both sectors, public and private, have experienced their fair share of successes and failures. Second, the two sectors have distinctly different missions. In simplistic terms, the mission of business is to maximize profit for shareholders; for government, the mission is to serve the greater public interest for its citizenry. Thus, two important distinctions to make are government seeks common wealth not private wealth and government is neither for profit nor nonprofit. It lies in between the two—not for profit.

Rosenbloom (1993) argued:

> The central problem of contemporary public administrative theory is that it is derived from three disparate approaches to the basic question of what public administration is. . . . These approaches are conveniently labeled "managerial," "political," and "legal." The managerial approach to public administration . . . stresses the importance of functional specification for efficiency. . . . The political approach . . . stresses the values of representativeness, political responsiveness, and accountability through elected officials to the citizenry. . . . The legal approach . . . embodies three central values. One is procedural due process. . . . A second value concerns individual substantive rights as embodied in evolving interpretations of the *Bill of Rights* and the *Fourteenth Amendment*. . . . Third, the judiciary values equity, a concept that like due process is subject to varying interpretation. (Rosenbloom 1993, 446–452)

There are additional approaches to public administration namely ethical, integrated/comprehensive, and historical (Lan and Anders 2000). Ergo, there are six approaches to public administration, including political, managerial, legal, ethical, integrated/comprehensive, and historical (Lan and Anders 2000, 158). The ethical approach requires public administrators to be cognizant of the consequences of administrative action. The integrated/comprehensive approach regards public administrators doing whatever is necessary to keep government functioning, and the historical approach traces contributions to the theoretical development of the field or to the practice of public administration (Lan and Anders 2000, 158). Another view of the political approach is public administrative issues as policymaking, power struggle, and resource allocation among different groups (Lan and Anders 2000, 158).

For our purposes, the political approach is the lens used here for understanding how citizens engage institutions to control their future or not.

CITIZEN PARTICIPATION MOVEMENT

Administrative agencies were established by law to execute specific public functions, for example, the Departments of Agriculture, Commerce, Defense, Education, Health, Homeland Security, Housing, Interior, Justice, and Labor. Since the 1930s, there have been policies aimed at involving the public in policy decisions. It is safe to conclude that some of these policies have not been successful. However, most recent U.S. administrations have attempted to engage the public with varying degrees of success. For the most part, citizen participation has operationalized as administrative agencies reaching out to what they deemed "affected citizens" in reference to a proposed policy or action.

Sherry Arnstein (1969) created a model depicting levels of citizen participation. Arnstein's "Ladder of Participation" had eight levels of participation for involvement of citizens in public decision-making ranging from nonparticipation to tokenism to citizen power (Arnstein 1969, 217). Citizen power was a redistribution of power that enabled citizens excluded from political and economic processes to be included in the future (Arnstein 1969, 216). There have been numerous models since then that have added value to understanding how citizens might engage government. Some of these were highlighted in chapter 2.

As the push for more citizen involvement progressed, Stenberg (1972) argued that "citizen participation" has evolved without a general consensus on who the "citizens" are and how they "participate." The major citizen participation developments occurred during three time periods: 1949–1963, 1964–1968, and 1969 to the present. The beginning of the citizen participation movement happened around the post–World War II period. He classified this period as the "nonindigenous citizen as advisor persuader," which consisted of "white planners, businessmen, civic leaders, and representatives of various groups and interests in the community, such as retired and manufacturing, construction, real estate, firefighters, labor, taxpayers, religion, and education". Stenberg labeled the period of 1964–1968 as "the indigenous citizen as partner adversary," meaning that "citizens were no longer predominantly affluent whites, instead they were mainly poor minority group members. They were neighborhood rather than citywide oriented" (Stenberg 1972, 190–192).

He argued that, "since the late 1960s, federal administrators have been giving increased attention to the problems and prospects of regional citizen participation" (Stenberg 1972, 193). Stenberg ascribed the period beginning in 1969 as "regionalism-decentralization" which he characterized as "citizens are playing a growing role in area wide planning conducted under the auspices of councils of government funded through the '701 program' [Section 701 of the Housing Act of 1954]" (Stenberg 1972, 193).

Rosenbaum (1976) stated:

> An increasing number of agencies now operate or have recently operated under mandates originating in Congress or within the agencies themselves which require federal officials to promote public involvement in administrative deliberations in a radically different manner from that once ordained by the *Administrative Procedures Act* [1946]. Until the mid 1960's, the Act . . . required only that agencies provide public notice and opportunity for public comment during rule making, that opportunities for public hearing exist. . . . *The Freedom of Information Act* [1966] . . . as amended, required additionally that government agencies provide the public, upon request, with papers, opinions, records, policy statements, and staff manuals not deemed highly sensitive. (Rosenbaum 1976, 355–356)

He argued:

> A major departure from the Act's procedures occurred through a variety of federal programs during the mid 1960s aimed specifically at the poor and underprivileged. First came the *Economic Opportunity Act (1964)* with its unprecedented Congressional Mandate . . . that the *Office of Economic Opportunity* achieved "maximum feasible participation" among the poor in the Community Action Programs. Next came the *Demonstration Cities Program (1966)* with its insistence that HUD "organize the unorganized"—the poor most often affected by the program. Unlike the earlier *Administrative Procedures Act*, these new programs identified a specific target population for involvement, mandated that responsible agencies actively createinvolvement procedures, and required participation at many stages in policy planning and implementation. While agencies are given an affirmative responsibility to encourage public involvement activities, the extent, location, and methods were left relatively vague. (Rosenbaum 1976, 357)

In 1983, Neuse argued:

> One school contends that citizens participation has been (or is potentially) an important stimulus for enhancing democratic norms and even for transferring effective power to the powerless. A second, contrarily, raises serious doubts regarding the efficiency of citizen participation programs, suggesting instead that such efforts often are failures. The citizen participation movement in the United States is less than 50 years old [less than 100 years today] and in many respects is a child of the welfare state it purports to challenge. Most scholars trace the ideology of citizen participation to the mid 1930's and the actions and rhetoric of new deal agencies, particularly the Department of Agriculture and the Tennessee Valley Authority. Aside from rather cursory and incomplete provisions regarding citizen involvement in bureaucratic policy matters in the *Administrative Procedures Act of 1946* . . . and in the urban renewal legislation in the 1950's, citizen participation was a dead letter. Since 1964, the year of the *Economic Opportunity* Act, the citizen participation movement has burgeoned. Community Action Agencies with citizen representatives are to be found in most large, medium, and small cities across the nation. (Neuse 1983, 294–298)

Today, the robustness of these agencies has waned over time.

Roberts (2004) asserted:

> Beginning with the presidency of Andrew Jackson, the 19th century saw a broadening of democratic practice both at state and national levels. Property qualifications were dropped and self-educated citizens, rather than elites, became part of the civil service. The first three decades of the 20th century witnessed the growth of other expressions of direct participation. Despite this apparent shift in emphasis from mandatory to advisable involvement, the 1970's were marked by an explosive growth in federally mandated citizen participation. The *Federal Advisory Committee Act of 1972* required citizen advisory boards throughout the Federal bureaucracy and encouraged the participation of organized interests. Demands for direct citizen participation in issues of basic welfare and quality of life expanded in the last two decades of the 20th century. A confluence of voices from students, union members, working and middle-class whites, government workers, environmentalists, feminists, and consumers amplified the movement. (Roberts 2004, 320–322)

According to Dudley et al. (2014) more controversial phrases on public participation were introduced into the fray including "potentially concerned public" (*UDAG* 1971 and *ISTEA* 1991) and the "best brains available" (House Committee on Government 1970). During the Obama administration, transparency in government was emphasized through his Open Government initiative. The primary focus was on making government information available to citizens and providing a platform for citizens to respond via technology and the Internet. Most recently, it appeared that technology and various forms of public meetings were frequently used methods for engaging the public as indicated in reports highlighted in chapter 4.

PUBLIC POLICYMAKING

In the U.S. polity, representative government is supposed to exist and function for the "common good." It appears that some citizens in the United States do not believe elected or appointed government officials represent their interests. Further, some citizens appear to be subsequently disengaged and all but shut out of the public policymaking processes. A critical mass of citizens argues that politicians, career bureaucrats, media, and experts shape public policy. Over the years, the visible and hidden policymakers have shaped policy solutions and policy alternatives. Some citizens assert that the interests served in this scenario are often different from their own. In fact, these citizens view this phenomenon as antidemocratic—primarily serving the interests and promoting the values of the power elite.

This perceived disengagement of some citizens from the public policymaking process is an important policy problem because citizens should be involved in creating policy alternatives affecting the general public. Government should be citizen driven, however, this cannot happen properly if citizens are not critical actors in policy development, policy alternatives, and policy implementation. Citizens should be afforded every opportunity to self-rule even in representative government.

A strong civil society is desirable in order to maintain a balance of order between citizen and state and to sustain a democratic republic such as the United States. How to maintain both social order and personal autonomy in one and the same society? In other words, how to construct a society that protects its members from one another—from civil war to violent crimes and do so without suppressing them (Etzioni 1996,1)? Etzioni (1996, 1) argued further that authentic communities, ones that are responsive to the "true needs" of all community members, reflect the appropriate balance of order and autonomy.

The task of government, as often proclaimed, is to serve or promote the public interest. Statutes sometimes include the public interest as a guide for agency action, as when the Federal Communications Commission is directed to license broadcasters for the "public interest, convenience, and necessity"

(Anderson 2006, 137). Citizen participation and engagement should be integral parts in guiding policy analysts in evaluating policy options.

Public policy affects us all in every facet of our lives whether we realize it or not. Literally, from pre-birth to the cradle to the grave, public policy prescribes what conditions are acceptable and appropriate standards for prenatal and postnatal care; how food and water are sanitized, processed, inspected, packaged, and delivered; occupational risks, hazards, and behaviors in the workplace; how we conduct ourselves in civil society; and last, how our bodily remains are properly disposed and preserved.

Beyond that point, citizens in democratic society should be informed about matters pertaining to them whether good or bad so they may act collectively. Citizens should engage in the public policymaking process to shape outcomes on matters affecting their lives. Citizens should be educated not only about the basics of civics but on their responsibilities and duties as an informed citizenry. It follows that an informed citizenry is an active populace capable of executing its civic duties.

In a representative government, such as the United States, government is supposed to be "of the people, by the people, and for the people." Citizens across the nation are alienated from, and distrustful of, government and elected officials. It is not enough for individuals to want to or try to participate as good citizens. Major institutions are setup to ignore and even frustrate civic engagement (Levine 2013,15). These citizens argue that their elected officials and their government no longer represent the public interest but rather their own interests and/or that of special interests.

Anderson postulated:

> Administrative agencies are often significantly involved in the formation of public policies. . . . Administration can make or break a law or policy that was made elsewhere. Administrative agencies are an important source of legislative proposals and ideas in the American political system. . . . Agencies also actively lobby and otherwise strive to win acceptance of legislation they favor or kill that which they oppose. (Anderson 2006, 53–54)

This type of influence occurs frequently on the state and national levels. Anderson argued

> In the twentieth and twenty-first centuries, the president, together with his chief aides and advisers in the Executive Office of the President, has been the leading source of initiative in forming major policy proposals (at the state level, the governors usually play the same role). Many policy proposals are developed by officials—both career and appointed—in the administrative departments and agencies . . . temporary organizations, sometimes called "ad-hocracies," may

> be established by the president to study particular policy areas and to develop policy proposals. . . . In the course of congressional hearings and investigations, through contacts with administrative officials and interest-group representatives, and on the basis of their own interests and activities, legislators receive suggestions for action on problems and formulate proposed courses of action. . . . Interest groups have a major role in policy formation, often going to the legislature with specific proposals for legislation. They may also work with executive and legislative officials to develop and enact an officially proposed policy, perhaps with some modifications to suit their interests. (Anderson 2006, 104–107)

The administration—the president and his appointees—is a particularly powerful agenda-setter, as are such prominent members of Congress as the party leaders and key committee chairs (Kingdon 2003, 199). Citizens are often left out of the policymaking processes. Consequently, there is a disconnect between citizens and policymakers.

TOP-DOWN VERSUS BOTTOM-UP OR BOTH?

In concert with the notion that citizens are disengaged from the public policymaking process is the idea that public policy is made at the highest levels of government and handed down to lower levels of government before engaging citizens, if at all, on the "street level." This top-down approach to conducting public affairs denies citizens full participation in their government. Conventional wisdom subscribes to this method of conducting public affairs. Others who represent grassroots prefer a bottom-up approach where policy alternatives emanate from the citizen level and rise to the top level of decision-making hierarchy.

Anderson argued:

> Most of the implementation studies take either a "top-down" or "bottom-up" approach. Top-downers focus on the actions of top-level officials. . . . Bottom-uppers contend that this approach gives too much attention to top-level officials and either ignores or underestimates the efforts of lower-level (or "street level") officials. (Anderson 2006, 202)

However, in any case, whether policy formation starts at the top or bottom does not ensure that the public interest will be better served. Experience has shown that the top-down bureaucratic approach to implementation has not always met with success, nor has turning over implementation to the service deliverers through a strictly bottom-up approach involving street-level bureaucrats and clients (Patton and Sawicki 1993, 307).

Nevertheless, there are advantages and disadvantages to both. In a representative government, citizens are supposed to be the highest-valued stakeholders of government. With respect to agenda setting, a top-down model of the executive branch seems to be surprisingly accurate. We discovered that the president can dominate his political appointees, and that appointees can dominate the career servants (Kingdom 2003, 31). What is happening with either approach is an assertion of power by the strong over and against the weak. Often the power elite suppresses the masses by manipulating or excluding their participation from public policymaking. The power elite is empowered to flex their muscles in this manner over the mass of citizens because they are lawmakers and policy influencers. They decide the allocation of resources stockpiled under their auspices.

The vast majority of American citizens-only recourses, which are significant, in regard to checks and balances in this instance, flow out of the US Constitution and Bill of Rights, that is, First Amendment rights of freedom of speech, to peaceably assemble and petition government for redress, and through the exercise of the right to vote as guaranteed by the Fifteenth Amendment, Nineteenth Amendment, Twentieth-Fourth Amendment, Twentieth-Sixth Amendment, and the Voting Rights Act of 1965 (as amended). Of course, their rights as citizens as guaranteed by the Fourteenth Amendment provide basic standing.

Some advantages of the "top-down" approach to policy development include ability of decision-makers to act quickly in a crisis such as the 9/11 terrorist attack; a cadre of qualified public servants were in place for decision-making purposes, that is, the president, cabinet members, staff members, and leaders of Congress. Others argue that there are apparent disadvantages inherent in this approach. Disadvantages that entail a majority of citizens are excluded from the policymaking process, decisions affecting the masses are decided by the power elite, and critical information of which citizens have a right to know may be withheld or distorted, for example, whether Iraq possessed weapons of mass destruction and what did the executive branch know prior to engaging in war against Iraq?

Still others assert that in a government like the United States a bottom-up approach offers advantages such as citizen engagement in decision-making that have impact upon their lives, trust level in government officials may rise, and democracy may strengthen as a result of inclusiveness in public policymaking processes. Citizen engagement fosters government legitimacy. Some critics of this approach argue that any associated advantages are outweighed by its shortcomings. These shortcomings include ordinary citizens not understanding the complex issues facing the nation, or even if they did understand, ordinary citizens do not have sufficient time or interest in public policy development, alternatives, or implementation. Others purport that in some cases a combination of both approaches may be the best course of action.

The Power Elite

C. Wright Mills (2000) argued that "the powers of ordinary men are circumscribed by everyday worlds in which they live, yet even in these rounds of jobs, family, and neighborhood they often seem driven by forces they can neither understand nor govern" (Mills 2000, 3). In other words, ordinary citizens are pawns of the power elite who control their lives, government, institutions, and corporations. Mills further asserted that "as the means of information and power are centralized, some men come to occupy positions in American society from which they can look down upon, so to speak, and by their decisions mightily affect, the everyday worlds of ordinary men and women" (Mills 2000, 303).

Unfortunately, this situation appears to be a frightening reality. Citizens have become less and less involved in determining their fates in America's democracy. If not by conspiracy or piracy then by other means, ordinary citizens have been reduced to little more than workers in a manufacturing plant making artificial products of which they neither own nor use, or reap much benefit other than their low wages and diminishing employee benefits. Mills posited that "the power elite is composed of men whose positions enable them to transcend the ordinary environments of ordinary men and women; they are in positions to make decisions having major consequences" (Mills 2000, 3). For examples, the power elite authorizes the levying of taxes, waging of war, enacting of laws governing housing, health, education, and welfare. The author argued, "They are in command of major hierarchies and organizations of modern society. They rule the big corporations. They run the machinery of state and claim its prerogatives. They direct military establishment" (Mills 2000, 4). Mills asserted, "Families and churches and schools adapt to modern life, governments and armies and corporations shape it; and as they do so, they turn these lesser institutions into means for their ends" (Mills 2000, 6).

In short, Mills posited that society is run by governmental, military, and corporate elites who manipulate other institutions to achieve their objectives. Mills argued that "the men of the circles composing this elite, severally and collectively, now make such key decisions; the decisions that they make and fail to make carry more consequences for more people than has ever been the case in the world history of mankind" (Mills 2000, 28). The decisions are made by the power elites with only tacit engagement of the citizens they suppose to represent. Under this scenario, the power elite may choose to declare war against any sovereign nation for whatever purpose it designs by launching a "pre-emptive strike" at any time it so desires without the consent or support of the governed. Or, as we have witnessed, on the domestic front the power elite can raise gasoline prices to such a high level as to alter driving and purchasing decisions and behaviors of ordinary citizens. This is a far different democracy than the Founders envisioned and, perhaps, a contributing factor to the disengagement of citizens from public life often perceived in American culture. However, one is baffled by these phenomena because the logical consequence of these events would be citizen's activism or revolt not apathy or withdrawal.

INTEREST GROUPS

What role do interests groups play in policymaking? Do these groups overshadow ordinary citizens? David Truman (1971) observed, "The fairly observant citizen sees various groups slugging it out with one another in pursuit of advantages from the government. Or he sees some of them cooperating with one another to their mutual benefit" (Truman 1971, 11). Are interest groups a threat to the system? If so, should these groups be controlled? Truman argued, "What we seek are correctives, protections, or controls that will strengthen the practices essential in what we call democracy and that will weaken or eliminate those that really threaten the system" (Truman 1971, 12). In Federalist #10, Madison stated there are two remedies for the mischiefs of a faction: removing it causes and controlling its effects (Truman 1971, 51). Truman asserted, "We need to re-examine our notions of how representative government operates in the United States before we can be confident of our statements about the effects of group activities upon it" (Truman 1971, 12). How resourceful are certain interest groups?

Truman posited:

> The considerable political importance of associations, that is, the groups formed around tangent relations, lies not only in their strong tendency to operate through or upon the institutions of government but in their stabilizing functions, in the larger resources of various kinds that they can command as compared with any of the participant elements, and in their great numbers in society. (Truman 1971, 43)

So, special interest groups provide a stabilizing effect on governmental institutions and supply a variety of resources. The big question is whether special interest groups exert undue influence on government. There is a perception that their influence is enormous to the extent of negating public interest.

To what extent are interest groups involved in American government? Truman argued:

> groups are a part of American politics . . . and they have always constituted an aspect of politics. In addition, they are so intimately related to the daily functioning of those constitutionalized [sic] groups—Legislature, chief executives, administrative agencies, and even courts—that make up the institution of government that the latter cannot adequately be described if these relationships are not recognized as the weft of the fabric. (Truman 1971, 46)

Truman asserted further that the "lobby" and the "pressure group" are familiar to many, "but they are accepted in the way that the typhoid bacillus is as an organism that is a feature of civilized existence but that must be eradicated if society is to develop and prosper" (Truman 1971, 46). Which type of interest group appeared to be more prevalent? Truman posited, "The increasing complexity of our society and the rapidity with which changes have occurred—creating greater intensity as well as frequency of disturbances—have made the association the most characteristic and pervasive sort of political interest group" (Truman 1971, 106). Although labor unions were chief among interest groups, their significance has waned over the past few decades. However, their mode of operation is worth noting as Truman stated:

> The tactics of opposing interest groups and the effectiveness of such traditional weapons as a monopoly of skill have led labor unions to make vigorous claims upon and through the institutions of government. Once made, such claims have been continued and expanded in order to strengthen and protect the measure of stability previously achieved. (Truman 1971, 107)

These groups still have influence and have evolved to coalesce with other affinity groups. Truman stated that "the activities of competing groups and the effectiveness of the weapons available to the associations when working alone have led these groups like the labor unions, to make increasing demands upon and through the government" (Truman 1971, 107).

What tactics do interest groups use to access government? Truman offered the notion that "the techniques utilized by interest groups and their 'members' in the legislature to enhance and exploit the degree of access that a group has been able to achieve are enormously complicated and varied" (Truman 1971, 391). Truman further stated, "Logrolling and alliances between groups—inevitable elements in a process that relies upon the device of majority rule to settle differences—become a means of compensating for the diffusion of power" (Truman 1971, 392).

Interest groups have found that such methods are powerful influencers of government action. Truman noted, "Collections of individuals interacting on the basis of shared attitudes and exerting claims upon other groups in society usually find in the institutions of government an important means of achieving their objectives" (Truman 1971, 502). However, these groups are never 100 percent unified in effort though they marshal a unified front. Truman posited that "organized interest groups are never solid and monolithic, though the consequences of their overlapping memberships may be handled with sufficient skill to give the organizations a maximum of cohesion" (Truman 1971, 510). In a philosophical yet real sense there is an unorganized interest among the masses that comes into play when driven to action by some element in the political atmosphere.

What are the dynamics of such a phenomenon? Truman argued, "In a relatively vigorous political system, however, these unorganized interests are dominant with sufficient frequency in the behavior of enough important segments of the society so that, despite ambiguity and other restrictions, both the activity and the methods of organized interest groups are kept within broad limits" (Truman 1971, 515). As one readily sees that policymaking is a complex and often ambiguous process with many actors and possible outcomes or alternatives. Truman asserted, "The process of accommodating group claims, moreover, does not necessarily produce a nice symmetry of public policy" (Truman 1971, 517). Interest groups no doubt have learned that the "squeaky wheel" usually gets greased. Truman noted, "No political party, regardless of its internal discipline, can be indifferent to the local impact of national decisions. That is, no elected official can ignore the possible reactions of voters, particularly groups of voters, in his constituency" (Truman 1971, 533).

CIVIC LIFE IN AMERICA

Do ordinary citizens have meaningful access to their government? Putnam asserted, "We have multiple avenues for expressing our rights" (2000, 31). Certainly, American citizens have many ways to access government but access alone does not translate into power to set agendas, shape policy decisions, or determine policy outcomes. Many public meetings with elected or appointed officials have the look and effect of being superficial and perfunctory.

Putnam posited that "voters are more likely to be interested in politics, to give to charity, to volunteer, to serve on juries, to attend community school board meetings, to participate in public demonstrations, and to cooperate with their fellow citizens on community affairs" (Putnam 2000, 35). If this is the case, why aren't voters more efficient at affecting policy decisions? Putnam argued, "Knowledge and interest in public affairs are critical preconditions for more active forms of involvement" (Putnam 2000, 35). Citizens still have common sense and are generally aware of public affairs as published or broadcasted through mass media. The author asserted, "Scandals and war can still arouse our attention, but generally speaking, fewer Americans follow public affairs now than did a quarter century ago" (Putnam 2000, 36). Putnam asserted, "Beyond party identification, at the grassroots level attending a campaign meeting or volunteering to work for a political party has become much rarer over the last thirty years" (Putnam 2000, 38). Could it be that the average citizen is more concerned with work and family matters and does not have the resources or time to devote to civic matters? With today's high unemployment rates and high costs of living, the average citizen may be consumed by the events of everyday life. Or, as Theda Skocpol retorted below, they are engaged in new ways.

Putnam argued, "Participation in politics is increasingly based on the checkbook, as money replaces time" (Putnam 2000, 40). The author asserted:

> Year after year, fewer and fewer of us took part in the everyday deliberations that constitute grassroots democracy. In effect, more than a third of America's civic infrastructure simply evaporated between the mid-1970s and the mid-1990s. . . . The changing pattern of civic participation in American communities over the last two decades has shifted the balance in the larger society between the articulation of grievances and the aggregation of coalitions to address those grievances. (Putnam 2000, 40–46)

Putnam argued:

> The more extreme views have gradually become more dominant in grassroots American civic life as more moderate voices have fallen silent. . . . It is commonly assumed that cynicism toward government has caused our disengagement from politics, but the converse is just as likely: that we have disaffected as we have dropped out, the real performance of government has suffered. (Putnam 2000, 342–347)

Berman (1997) posited that "cynicism is present in about one-third of all cities with populations over 50,000, and that about one-quarter of these have widespread, 'ardently' cynical attitudes" (Berman 1997, 111). Putnam observes that the social fabric of civil society in America has worn apart as measured by eroding social capital over the last generation. The General Survey revealed that at all education levels of American society, and counting all sorts of group memberships, Americans have been dropping out in droves, not merely from political life, but from organized community life more generally (Putnam 2000, 63).

Putnam (2000, 46) argues that since the mid-1960s, Americans are less likely to voice views publicly by running for office or writing Congress or the local newspaper, less interested in politics and public affairs, less likely to vote, less likely to attend public meetings, less engaged in party politics, political, and civic organizations. Hypothetically, it follows that citizens may be less likely to feel the excitement and empowerment of general elections, a patriotic duty to paying taxes, a deep sense of caring and belonging to community, and a passionate desire for voluntary associations or selfless pursuit of public purposes.

Is there a different explanation of the current state of civic America?

Theda Skocpol (2003) argues:

> Where once cross-class voluntary federations held sway, national public life is now dominated by professionally managed advocacy groups without chapter members. . . . No longer are supreme acts of national citizenship . . . understood as going hand in hand with active participation in voluntary associations . . . that the delinking of civic engagement from politics and national government takes on an even harder edge among contemporary US conservatives. (Skocpol 2003, 7–8)

She argues:

> Early twenty-first century Americans live in a diminished democracy, in a much less participatory and more oligarchical managed civic world. . . . Many thinkers misdiagnose the civic challenges America faces today, for they have forgotten that national community, active government, and democratic mobilization are all vital to creating and sustaining a vibrant civil society. . . . In the US, democratic governance and civic voluntarism developed together. . . . The professionally managed organizations that dominate American civic life today are . . . less democratic and participatory than the pre-1960s membership federations they displaced. (Skocpol 2003, 11–13)

She asserts that "As the worriers use survey data to show that America since the 1950s are joining and participating less, the optimists document the increase in organizational establishments since the 1960s" (Skocpol 2003, 14). Skocpol posits:

> In an era when civic leaders are organizing and running very different kinds of voluntary organizations from those that held sway before the 1960s—and a time when Americans mean very different things by civic involvement than they once did—it is simply not enough to count affiliations with vague types of groups or to ask people how many "community meetings" they have attended in the past year. We must not simply count group membership, but look into the various kinds of associations that have flourished in various times and circumstances. We must aim to explain how US voluntary associations have changed

> over time and consider what difference the changes have made for our democracy. (Skocpol 2003, 17)

Skocpol asserts:

> Professionally run advocacy groups and nonprofit institutions now dominate civil society, as people seek influence and community through a very new mix of largely member-less voluntary organizations. . . . In the 1960s and 1970s massive social movements bypassed federated member associations and set the stage for the proliferation of new kinds of professionally run civic undertakings. . . . The largest membership groups of the 1950s were old line and well established, with US founding dates ranging from 1733 for the Masons to 1939 for the United Methodist Women. (Skocpol 2003, 127–129)

She argues that "Contemporary Americans are not simply joining old associations less frequently than their forebears did. They are also organizing to an extraordinary degree, and engaging public affairs in very new ways" (Skocpol 2003, 175–76).

Have citizens ever held government accountable? In postmodernity, perhaps the protest movements of the 1960s and 1970s were effective at attracting elected officials' attention, and their legislative and administrative responses to change status quo. However, these tactics appear less effective today. Perhaps government has morphed in such a way as to become immune to citizen complaint, interest, or protest. Therefore, government has freed itself to exercise the will of the power elite without regard for the "public will." Maybe, the American republic has grown into maturity. Perhaps, the republic has got too big and cumbersome to deal effectively with public functions or issues affecting ordinary citizens save inaugurations, celebrations, and state funerals. Is American democracy dead? Is there a conspiracy against ordinary citizens?

In 2004, Crenson and Ginsberg argued, "American democracy is not dead. It has, however, undergone a transfiguration, and so has the American citizenship. These changes do not come from some vast conspiracy to deprive the general public of its place in politics" (Crenson and Ginsberg 2004, 2). Perhaps, it is impossible to prove conspiracy however this notion should not be considered flippantly.

They asserted:

> The proliferation of opportunities for individual access to government has substantially reduced the incentives for collective mobilization. For many ordinary Americans, this means that it has become standard practice to deal with government as individuals rather than members of a mobilized public. At the

> same time, Americans of more than ordinary political status find that they can use the market, courts, administrative procedures, and other political channels to achieve their ends without organizing the support of a political constituency. (Crenson and Ginsberg 2004, 3)

Crenson and Ginsberg posited:

> Rather than expand the range of public benefits to broaden their support base; elites promote the private market as a better source than government for education, health, welfare, and old-age benefits. Rather than expand the base of the federal pyramid through voter mobilization, elites disparage representative institutions as grid locked and ineffectual. (Crenson and Ginsberg 2004, 5)

Amusedly, if the power elite working through public officials could have their agendas effectuated without vetting them before citizens then these elites could pursue other paths that offer fewer roadblocks and shorter distances to their ends.

What is government doing to promote good citizenship? The authors argued, "Citizenship is no longer about the collective activity of governing" (Crenson and Ginsbert 2004, 6). They asserted, "Students are urged to produce public services that a voting public once demanded from government. . . . Lessons in service have supplanted training for sovereignty" (Crenson and Ginsberg 2004, 6). Crenson and Ginsberg posited, "American institutions operate increasingly to disaggregate and de-politicize the demands of citizens" (Crenson and Ginsberg 2004, 14). Is this statement an admission of conspiracy? Maybe?

The authors asserted that "the 'reinvention' of American government has reinvented citizens as customers. . . . It is promoting arrangements for policy implementation that encourage individual choice rather the articulation of public interests" (Crenson and Ginsberg 2004, 14). "The political theory of reinvention, founded on a faith in individual self-interest as the engine that drives social good, in fact acts to deny the ideal of citizenship" (deLeon and Denhardt 2000, 94). Crenson and Ginsberg posited, "Government has begun to privatize not only many of its own functions but the public itself. American politics has entered an era of personal democracy" (Crenson and Ginsberg 2004, 14). However, the public is not monolithic. The American public encompasses a broad spectrum of cultures and experiences. The vast majority of American citizens are trapped in the lower middle class and lowest echelon of society without sufficient resources to exercise choice. Thus, politics in America may have entered into this personalized era but the jury is still out on the public though some citizens are behaving like consumers.

CITIZENS AS COPRODUCERS

Coproduction is synergy between what government does and what citizens do (Ostrom 1996, 1079). As I mentioned in chapter 1, citizens have capacity to solve public problems and the ability to work with institutions to solve problems. I add here that public administrators should work with citizens to solve public problems. No major public problem should be implemented or action taken without effective engagement of the affected public. The government should work with citizens to produce public goods and services. Inspired by Abe Lincoln's Gettysburg address and the spoken words "government of the people, by the people, and for the people," David Mathews ponders, why not government "with" the people (Mathews forthcoming, 5).

The people, as citizens, are seen as moral and political actors capable of ethical judgment. Their views are valued on an equal basis and they have not only a right but also a responsibility to act in ways that they believe will realize the common wealth of society and democratic decision-making (Seddon 2004, 173). Bramson (2005, 24) posits that citizens have become much more actively involved in making public decisions and solving public problems. She argues that this increased involvement seems to be happening for a number of reasons, including more legislation requiring public participation, citizen demands for involvement in decisions that affect their lives, and changing professional values on the part of public officials (Bramson 2005, 24). Bramson posits that there is no simple "how to" guide for deciding when to involve the public, whom to involve in public decisions, which public participation tools and processes to employ, and how to interpret and utilize the public input (Bramson 2005, 31). She argues further that too often public involvement programs are initiated with high hopes and good intentions, only to lead to costly and time-consuming dead-ends, which are frustrating for everyone involved (Bramson 2005, 31). I argue that public servants have a duty to include citizens at every stage of the policymaking process. In the final analysis, government is all about the people.

Roberts (1997, 126) asserts that the deliberative process requires public executives not simply to discover what people want for themselves and then to implement the best means for satisfying these wants. She argues it is to provide the public with alternative visions of what is desirable and possible, to stimulate discussion, to provoke reexamination, to broaden the range of potential responses, and to deepen society's understanding.

Civic engagement and political participation are also considered important sources of civic learning, particularly in relation to the acquisition of civic and political skills (Schugurensky 2003, 325). Fine and Harrington (2004, 349) argue that one way to gauge the health of civil society is to measure the proliferation of small groups. Societies in which there is a high degree of civic engagement require a high density of small groups to facilitate debate and advocacy to produce collective action. Representative government requires public servants to act on behalf of citizens as trustees of the commonwealth. Democracy requires citizens to act in the public interest.

SUMMARY

It is the duty of public servants to view "citizens as assets as opposed to deficits" (a phrase often used by John L. McKnight and John P. Kretzmann) and as rightful guardians of the democratic regime. Therefore, citizens are entitled to coproduce public goods and services. Public administration is what governments do or do not. Citizen participation has been promoted since the 1930s. Special interests and other organized groups have more influence on government than unorganized citizens. The question of whether citizens are less active today in civic life is debatable. Whether decisions are made from the top or bottom may depend on the problem at hand. Citizens as producers or coproducers often depend on the value they bring to the table. However, citizens must be treated as coproducers.

So, public administrators and citizens have obligations for making democratic institutions work to serve the common good. If citizens are the true owners of government and the highest-valued stakeholders of the republic then their voices must be heard at all levels of decision-making. If otherwise, the regime established would be something other than government of, by, and for the people.

Citizens and community members have important roles to play in ensuring that the republic in which they reside lives up to its constitutive and democratic ideals. Their capacities and fortitude are keys to forging their mutual concerns and compassing their common destiny.

Chapter 4 explores more cases to shed light on the numerous ways that institutions work with citizens. These cases demonstrate the challenges of democratic values in a mature republic.

Chapter 4

Coproduction with Federal Agencies, a Municipality, and a Nonprofit Organization

This first set of four research reports addressed the question of aligning the work of institutions with the work of citizens by exploring coproduction. The researchers were searching for evidence of citizen interaction with federal agencies, a municipality, and a nonprofit organization. In evaluating these reports, special attention was given to democratic practices as a method for gauging citizen engagement.

FEDERAL AGENCIES

Larkin Dudley et al. (2014) examined four federal agencies to determine the extent to which they collaborate with and involve the public. Researchers sought to discover evidence of coproduction between administrative agencies and citizens. Their report included results of interviews with seventeen federal officials and a summary of policies of the four agencies under investigation: the Department of Education, the Environmental Protection Agency, the Department of Health and Human Services, and the Department of Housing and Urban Development. Passages from the report, shown below, describe the study in brief:

> In our review of participation practices, we found diverse methods used to reach citizens, a focus on inclusiveness, the belief in the four agencies that their approach to public engagement was unique to their agencies, and recognition of the importance of community knowledge in complex processes of engagement.
>
> When asked how they might improve participation, interviewees mentioned more time to implement programs, more funding (especially in a time of declining resources, with competing priorities among smaller funding pools), and

the need for specific funding for public participation in grants and other programs. A few respondents mentioned the need to involve the community early, before major decisions are made. Some recommended a greater emphasis on methods of communication, and others stressed the importance of training technical experts to work with communities. Finally, some interviewees spoke of the need to convince senior leadership that conventional participation formats are no longer working. Unfortunately, many respondents lamented that they are doing a poor job of evaluating participation processes and learning from those evaluations: activities that are frequently expensive and time-intensive, but which could aid them in internal discussions on the importance of high-quality participation. . . .

Different laws, projects, and initiatives that claim to promote participation at the federal level do not seem to support one another; in fact, they often seem to be based on very different assumptions about citizenship and democracy. . . . Federal participation is made confusing by the fact that many of the "citizens" being engaged particularly in local policy decisions, would be better described as "stakeholders.". . .

One thing that did not often come up in these interviews—at least, until we brought it into the picture—was Open Government Directive. . . . [The Directive and the accompanying Open Government National Action Plan], issued by President Obama on his first day in office, was intended to clarify, organize, and catalyze public participation. The Directive set out transparency, participation, and collaboration as the cornerstones of open government. . . . Unfortunately, most of the strategies incorporated in the . . . document . . . have proven insufficient to the task.

Overall, we found examples of programs involved in the first stages of co-design, i.e. in soliciting the opinions and suggestions, primarily from stakeholders, on how to improve policy and programs. However, we did not find many instances where federal agencies were involving citizens in . . . coproduction . . . these agencies, and the Administration as a whole, have been more involved in promoting transparency, and have not yet attempted to conduct public participation in ways that would build long-term political capital and public will for engagement and its outcomes.

Generally, I am not surprised by these findings. I am struck, however, by the finding that there is inconsistency within and among federal agencies with regard to their understanding and application of public participation policies. Different laws, projects, and initiatives appeared not to support one another. Further, each of the four agencies appeared to think their public participation efforts were unique. One would hope that these agencies would improve their communication with one another with respect to their experiences—both successes and failures—in this area.

In some cases, researchers found that experts and agency representatives decided which comments from the public were relevant. While administrative agencies have multiple ways of communicating with citizens and recognizing the importance of their knowledge, they are also fearful that not enough resources are devoted to these efforts and convinced that senior leadership needs to change its routines.

The research did not reveal any evidence of coproduction. Obama's Open Government Initiative and National Action Plan appeared to have little if any effect on public participation. What Dudley et al. found were federal agencies involved in promoting transparency while paying little attention to effective public participation. It appeared that public administrators blame their lackluster commitment to effective public participation on inadequate funding and leadership.

Finally, the question of who the "public" actually is arose frequently in these interviews. The research suggested that those who federal agencies considered as "the public" would be better described as "stakeholders." Since there appeared to be minimum public participation with these administrative agencies, specific democratic practices could not be found.

Six More Federal Agencies

In a second report on federal agencies, Larkin Dudley, Noel Gniady-Banford, and Kathryn Webb Farley (2016) interviewed a total of forty-four officials from six more agencies in their search for evidence of coproduction. These agencies, which included the Departments of Agriculture, Energy, Interior, Justice, Transportation, and Homeland Security, were naming and framing problems and issues in a variety of ways, none of which included the public. The following passages from the report describe findings of the research:

> Based on the [Kettering Foundation] model of six practices of public life (naming, framing, deliberating, identifying and committing resources, organizing action, and learning), we find that agencies encourage the practices to varying degrees, as shaped by the broad concepts of the agency's context, definitions of engaged publics, and processes.
>
> Naming the problem is the first step in developing a collective understanding of any issue. . . . None of the interviews indicated any conscious effort for public involvement in the naming of problems. . . . Further, and perhaps most significant, much of the naming came from Congress.
>
> After the issue is named and framed, our interviewees indicated differences in what may expand or limit options considered in deliberation, as well as determine who is included to make decisions deliberatively. . . . Our interviews suggested that agencies actively identify and commit resources to better engage

> the public. In particular, to better inform and engage the public, agencies follow official processes to provide and gather information, such as notice and comment periods; rely on the media to disseminate information; and distribute technical information based on their expertise. . . . There was evidence that using these resources resulted in organizing action that built relationships and trust between the federal agency and the public. Interviewees were cognizant of the importance of trust to promote working together as well as to understanding different points of views. . . . It seems that some in federal agencies promote learning as a community, not only as reflection on specific instances, but rather by providing resources such as guides or playbooks that promote further public engagement.
>
> Obstacles to implementing these six practices include lack of resources, organizational attributes and processes, communication, organizational environment, differential access, characteristics of citizens, and lack of incentives. The large scale of federal agency responsibilities inhibits efforts to even consider deliberative democracy. The expectations of public engagement at the federal level are tempered by political and legal federal structure and the resulting widespread belief and practice in devolving participation to state and local level. Further since many decisions involve technical questions, agencies tend to filter out value-based comments in favor of legal or scientific comments.
>
> Ways to overcome obstacles include citizens as participants in official processes, changing internal processes, and increasing training. . . . Furthermore, developing networks and collaboration with stakeholders, media, and citizens and creating the capacity to interact with these entities are important. Working through networks and collaboration to engage the public may help to improve the practices of public life despite the obstacles.
>
> Ultimately, meaningful deliberation among citizens as well as among citizens and governmental institutions at all levels may require a more refined concept of who citizens are and what they can and should do.

Clearly, public administrators encouraged democratic practices, and almost all of those interviewed recognized the value of public participation but, for the most part, tended not to implement these concepts in their daily routines. With notable exceptions, one-way e-government methods seem to be favored over deliberative ones. It appeared that unless required by specific mandates, agencies tended to devolve any deliberative efforts to local and state levels.

In the liberal days of the 1960s and 1970s, administrative agencies at the state and local levels felt compelled to engage with citizens, or were at least interested in doing so, and federal agencies in many instances supported these efforts. In the last twenty years, however, the emphasis on e-government at the federal level has changed the idea of public participation. Instead, based on findings from both reports, it appeared that federal agencies (at least the ten that were investigated in this study) have emphasized transparency, information sharing, and one-way communication with citizens on specific concerns. Needless to say, democratic practices do not have a chance in administrative agencies if administrators and citizens cannot make things happen and if neither the broader society nor agency culture supports such endeavors. There may be hope for change, of course, in the participatory efforts exercised by administrators in some of the agencies studied by the researchers.

The Los Angeles Fire Department

Tia Gaynor (2015) conducted a study of the Los Angeles Fire Department (LAFD) to ascertain whether a particular program was coproductive. The program involved the cooperation between the LAFD and former gang members associated with the Professional Community Intervention Training Institute (PCITI) in more effectively delivering fire and rescue services in south LA communities. Gaynor describes the program as follows:

> The LAFD recognized that, as an organization, it was not effectively meeting the needs of all of the residents they serve. As a result, it embarked upon a unique relationship with former gang members (OGs) where bi-directional education led to drastic changes in the services provided to south L.A. communities.
>
> The LAFD partnered with PCITI to co-jointly train one another to educate and prepare for fire and rescue activities in the community. The fire department trained community members on life saving techniques and policies and community members educated the firefighters on gang culture and behaviors. What appeared to be unlikely bedfellows has proven to be a good partnership for delivery of fire and rescue services in a disparate community. Once reluctant firefighters were fearful of answering calls of emergencies in the neighborhood now bravely arrive on the scene with the assistance of OGs. Evident within the perspectives of both LAFD firefighters and interventionists is that deliberation and dialogue were at the crux of this partnership, serving to promote and enhance coproduction. The discord that existed between residents and the LAFD has been subdued because of the co-productive relationship between LAFD and PCITI, the bi-directional education and training provided, and each organization serving as a liaison when needed. Successively, trust between all parties has begun to develop. It, therefore, seems evident that in the case of LAFD and PCITI the presence of deliberation and dialogue enhanced, rather than stunted, coproduction.
>
> Although this partnership has proven to be successful and made tremendous strides in increasing trust, reducing discord, and better meeting community needs, challenges remain. Training for firefighters remains sporadic and is not ongoing or institutionalized. The partnership continues due to the two pioneers

> who began the initiative. Since the collaboration has not been formally integrated into the operations of both organizations, it may cease to exist after each pioneer is no longer affiliated with his respective organization.
>
> Firefighters are regularly transferred in and out of station; therefore, individuals who have recently been transferred into a station in south L.A., may not have received training. Without consistently offering training to new firefighters in south L.A. stations and new interventionists, the historical issues that existed may cycle back, negating the work that has already been done. The sporadic training of firefighters combined with a revolving door at fire stations prevents sustained relationships between firefighters and community residents. This . . . serves as an obstacle for residents, other than interventionists, to engage in long-standing coproductive partnerships.
>
> Despite these challenges, this example of coproduction has demonstrated its ability to have real-world impacts that strengthen communities, their interactions with public administrators, and allow public organizations to serve communities in efficient, effective and equitable ways.

The LAFD had an incentive to engage with citizens that grew out of fear for their own safety when arriving on the scene of an emergency in crime-ridden neighborhoods. The unwritten policy exercised by fire and rescue workers was to stage two blocks away until cleared to approach the scene.

Although evidence of coproduction was found between the citizens and the LAFD participating in this program there appears to be little evidence that democratic practices are used otherwise to solve problems faced by this community. Furthermore, since this example of coproduction is not institutionalized it may disappear after its two founders are no longer active in the program. Nonetheless, this is a good example of coproduction. It appears to be worthy of support by the LAFD and communities in the service area. Imagine the impact on LA residents if this kind of partnership was adopted and instituted throughout the city. It may be, of course, that if we searched the city to discover how other citizens solved their problems with the resources available to them we might find more evidence of democratic practices in play.

Faith in Florida

Brandi Blessett (2016) set out to ascertain whether coproduction existed between citizens and a nonprofit organization. Her target was Faith in Florida, an NGO that has developed a model for engaging the community in public problem solving. Her attention was directed to Faith in Florida's efforts to restore the rights of persons formerly imprisoned in the state. The passage below provides a summary of the research.

Rights restoration emerged as a topic for Faith in Florida when organizers met with residents of the Parramore neighborhood, a historically Black area in Orlando.

At least half of the residents in the discussion had failed to secure meetings with the City Commissioner because of criminal backgrounds. Residents were stigmatized and barred from the rights and privileges of full citizenship. This kind of stigmatization reduced formerly incarcerated persons to second-class citizens as they could not bear arms, vote, or secure gainful employment. So, Faith in Florida engaged these residents in campaigns to "ban the box" and restore voting rights. The campaigns were successful (though not entirely) in changing the policy of having job applicants to answer the question regarding being convicted of a felony; and having the governor to change the policy on restoration of voting rights.

In Florida, disenfranchisement reveals a disproportionate racial burden that threatens the legitimacy of public institutions and administration alike. Millions of people and hundreds of communities are impacted by mass incarceration, recidivism, and disenfranchisement.

Faith institutions, the nonprofit sector, community leaders, and citizens can only do so much. Government must be willing to partner with and work toward equitable outcomes for all of America's citizens. The stigma of incarceration should never render someone a permanent second-class citizen in his or her respective society. Punishment should not continue for a lifetime after a debt is paid to society. People should not feel as if there is more to life in prison than out in society.

This is a heartbreaking but true reality for many returning citizens. Rights restoration is just one aspect of a larger problem. Individuals, families, and communities are becoming part of an underclass that exists at the margins of society. Disenfranchisement has been a long-standing practice and the reality is that people are not better off by being stigmatized as outcasts. Some scholars argue that re-enfranchisement might encourage rehabilitation because: . . . respect for the law and the legal system may well depend, on some measure, on his ability to participate in the system. Moreover . . . the loss of citizenship rights [including] the right to vote . . . inhibits reformative efforts. If corrections is to reintegrate the offender into free society, the offender must retain all attributes of citizenship (Hull 2006, 44–45). Ultimately, we have decades' worth of evidence that suggests disenfranchisement does more harm than good. Therefore, if the United States ever wants to truly live up to its ideals, then rethinking the dimensions of citizenship has to be a top priority. In the end, though rights restoration was important for residents, moving forward the primary issues were housing and employment.

This report is an example of how a nonprofit organization can engage ordinary citizens in complementary action. Citizens worked with the NGO to control their common destiny. Nevertheless, perhaps the question is not what institutions can do for—or even with—citizens, but what citizens can do for themselves. What can citizens do to change institutional norms and behaviors? What can citizens do to control their collective future? Are citizens willing to exercise specific democratic practices? Citizens may be barred from controlling their future once incarcerated, stripped of basic civil rights and returned to society without full legal citizenship status. In this case, though, former prisoners exercising democratic practices did have some impact on their common destiny.

PUBLIC PARTICIPATION IN MUNICIPAL GOVERNMENT

The second set of four reports, written by Kara Lindaman (2015, 2017), Marijoan Bull (2017), and Ellen Knutson (2014), explored the extent to which ordinary citizens were engaged in public decision-making in municipal government and how effective their participation was. Under the microscope were small cities in Ohio, Massachusetts, and Minnesota, and the 49th Ward in Chicago. Once again, special attention was given to democratic practices as indicators of the level of citizen engagement.

Fairborn, Ohio, and a "Sense of Community"

The City of Fairborn, which had identified slum landlords as a public problem, partnered with Kara Lindaman in 2015 to organize public forums. Citizens participating in the forums, however, framed the issues somewhat differently and renamed the problem as Fairborn's "sense of community." Lindaman, who reported on the outcome of the citizen/government interaction in Fairborn, summed up her findings as follows:

> Citizen engagement is not only a way to dwindle the institutional legacies of a client-centered paternalistic and passive approach to service delivery but it is also a way to increase the level of trust in institutions and public service. . . . The active role of the citizen, rather than the consumer or the client, determines the ethos of the community and the health of the democracy or public.
>
> Trust in community, trust in neighbors, and trust in government are highly intertwined and interdependent. Putnam (2015) exposes this decline in trust in Port Clinton, Ohio, which leads not only to economic decline but rather exacerbates gross economic inequality and deteriorates further the sense of community and social connectedness. His findings may be applied in similar ways to his neighbor, Fairborn. However, from these findings and experience, the

stark distinction between Port Clinton and Fairborn is an identified intentional paradigm shift through transformational leadership and deliberative practice, which may indeed provide the necessary optimism and action to quell the tides of democratic decline and inequality exposed by Putnam.

Of course, it is not simple or easy. The leadership evident through this process in Fairborn is justifiably transformational, engaged, innovative, and empowering (Raelin 2003) coins this new form of leadership as "leaderful leadership" or leadership which is concurrent, collective, collaborative, and compassionate (Minor 2004). Indeed, the city manager of Fairborn is a purposeful leader, who enables connections and empowers citizens for community building and democratic engagement. Whether this is a "leaderful leader" or a "deliberative entrepreneur" (Fagotto and Fung 2009), this democratic leadership in both theory and practice deserves recognition. As the forum introduced democratic deliberation, the movement towards "embedded deliberation" (see Fagotto and Fung 2009) demands a citizen-leader or a citizen-city manager.

As the first intentional democratic deliberation, the forum begins the process towards hopeful and eventual embeddedness, and final paradigm shift or culture change toward coproduction and civic governance. As an outsider, the researcher provided the optimal vantage point to understand the underlying basic assumptions and patterns of behaviors and expectations unknowingly guiding untrusted practices in Fairborn. With the dismal diagnosis and dissolving public trust, a culture shift is necessary. The practice of democratic deliberation for shared civic governance or coproduction is a tremendous step in the right direction.

In sum, coproduction in local government and communities were operationalized through a study of Fairborn, Ohio, with an introduction to the democratic deliberative process through a forum on the sense of community. Concern gathering commenced in the intention of broaching wicked problems over what kind of community citizens want. The value of democratic deliberation was definitively discovered and its effects towards civic governance and coproduction are prime for measurement and evaluation. This pilot was a demonstrated start to a potentially successful future. Already the City of Fairborn continues to embrace and employ the process and terms of deliberation shared through the forums in their civic engagement. The efforts of Fairborn citizens should be applauded and documented as their democratic experiment continues.

In this case City Hall named the problem "slum landlords" because of a number of complaints and citations. But when the citizens assembled to deliberate about the problem they saw the issue in a broader context. Seeking evidence of coproduction, what the researcher found was City Hall reaching out to citizens and beginning the process of trust building. Among other things, this case turned out to be a lesson that once more illuminated the fact that ordinary citizens view and name problems and frame issues differently than do professionals or experts.

Since this report, the citizen-centered city manager has left the employ of the city. Fairborn may have continued its experimentation with deliberative public forums, or defaulted back to business as usual. Without ongoing research in this city, it is impossible to assess its level of engagement with specific democratic practices.

Safe Routes to School in Springfield, Massachusetts

Marijoan Bull (2017) explored efforts to initiate a Safe Routes to School (SRTS) program in West Springfield, Massachusetts. She examined how deliberative forums were used to make collective decisions. This study reflected on how the integration of parent dialogues, designed with deliberative features, affected and shaped a set of recommendations for action. Bull describes the research below:

> Focusing on children in kindergarten through grade eight, (SRTS) seeks to make the trip to and from school, safe, healthy, green, and fun. By increasing the number of students walking or biking to and from school, more students are incorporating physical exercise into their day, fewer cars are idling at schools, and social connections have the potential to increase. . . . West Springfield is a community of just under 30,000 located in western Massachusetts' Hampden County. The community is predominantly suburban in character, with some remaining rural sections. It is located along the west bank of the Connecticut River, west of the regional urban center of Springfield, Massachusetts. . . . The work focused on two elementary schools within West Springfield. . . . The major take-away from this effort was how the parents (particularly at the Memorial School PTO meeting) renamed and reframed the issue. . . . Parents at the PTO meeting spoke about the trip to and from school, but more importantly they renamed the issue as one of safe access to recreation and community spaces. . . .
>
> While SRTS evaluated conditions during arrival and dismissal, the parents noted crossing guards are not present during after school hours, weekends, and throughout the summer—times when children are still crossing the busy intersections.
>
> This is a good example of how naming a problem can limit solutions, and why having citizens directly involved in the definition stage is critical. . . . By reframing the issue in a broader way—situating it in local realities—parents advocated for year-round safety improvements that fit their neighborhood. The SRTS methodology alone would have left the analysis at finding the conditions adequate, as crossing guards are in place for children at these busy intersections.

> In addition, parents expanded the conversation from the data that showed few children rode their bikes to school, to the reality of children riding bikes at home. Parents voiced concern that safety at home on the streets of the neighborhood should be considered too—not just making the trip to and from school by bike. Parents were speaking about something dear to them—the safety of children—and it was clear this mattered. When considering this subject, they did not limit themselves to the routes to and from school. Another characteristic of parents' reframing, is their ability to see the connections between the initial concentrated inquiry and the complexities of development. Without prompting from the data collected, parents spoke about the commercial traffic and dangerous conditions in the area related to the pattern of homes interspersed with businesses. . . . It is anticipated that the two actions parents determined as helpful—the safety improvements and more traffic enforcement—will be pursued by the respective town authorities, the Public Works Department and the Police Department.

This study illustrated, once again, the ways that citizens view the universe differently than do professionals. Citizens tend to see specific public problems in the larger context and almost always in terms of how these problems and their solutions affect those things they care about most. It appears that unless certain democratic practices are injected into their dealings with the public, the professionals tend to go about their business as usual. It is also apparent that when citizens engage in the efforts needed to control their future the outcomes and consequences become more acceptable and legitimate.

Winona, Minnesota, and Public Decision-Making

Winona, Minnesota, was the subject of a case study by Kara Lindaman (2017) in which she compares and contrasts the city's closed decision-making process in 2015–2016 with a more democratic approach used in 2016–2017. Her study explored ways that citizens and public officials could find common ground on transportation and pedestrian safety issues in the city. She describes the research in the passage below:

> Transportation in the city of Winona provides the perfect storm, which exposes the complexities or "wickedness" of the issue and complicates it further with the overlapping jurisdictions, including but not limited to Winona State University (WSU), the city of Winona, the state of Minnesota and all of the relevant "publics" or constituencies. Truly this is a public problem deserving of greater scrutiny and understanding, where complementary production is a necessity rather than a choice. . . . In March 2016, the third person in six weeks was killed by a train in Winona. . . . A few months earlier a WSU student was killed by a train.

What is most striking about these accidents is that they occurred at intersections where many students [frequently] cross.

This study seeks to compare and contrast the closed decision-making process used in 2015–16 to that of a more democratic, deliberative, and transparent process in 2016–17 to fully name, frame, and find common ground on issues that involve transportation, and city and university safety and well-being. . . . The [2015–2016] naming and framing process is studied in contrast to previous decision-making processes . . . to measure the effects toward increased trust between public administrators (city and university) and citizens . . . to address transportation and safety needs.

Combined with the preparation of an issue guide along the model of the National Issues Forums and completed at a Center for Public Life, the continued work of the Pedestrian Safety Committee is observed and recorded to get a sense of the action(s) and work done. This is very important given the nature of committees formed to solve problems before the democratic sense of the community is collected and evaluated. . . . [An earlier initiated] tunnel project is an excellent example of a solution to pedestrian safety offered by the university, without city and/or student input and, consequently support. While it took multiple stakeholders to receive the federal dollars, it is deemed a solely WSU initiated project to ensure its anticipated expansion and growth, and to provide the safety assurance to students and their families.

[In] the spirit of democracy and civic engagement, concern gathering and definition in the creation of an issue guide was completed by students. The three approaches are as follows: personal responsibility, increased regulation, and transportation education.

In the study of transportation and pedestrian safety in Winona, Minnesota, the politics-administration dichotomy is criticized not because information asymmetry no longer exists but because deliberative democracy and engaged participation has resurfaced in the midst of confused and contentious politics. As the American political system and institutions are tested in unanticipated ways, this study finds regular citizens, even the "smallest" of all in Winona—students—refining and employing their civic skills to use the tools of deliberative democracy to change community for the better. While it is uncertain what the sustained impact of their democratic deliberative efforts will be, students as citizens are establishing policy innovation and a cultural trend to be the agents of democracy in issues that matter the most to them and to community.

In sum, Winona State University decided to construct a tunnel at the site of repeated deadly train accidents as a remedy to the problem without engaging either the public or its own student body. Later, the students engaged in deliberative forums, naming and framing the problem and offering their own views on how it would be solved. They crafted three options: students should take responsibility, government should provide more regulations, and students should be educated on transportation safety. In short, the students took control of the problem and decided how the problem would be named, framed, and resolved. This is a case where students took charge of their future using several democratic practices. As with all such cases, ongoing study is necessary to gauge the long-term effect of deliberative practices on community.

Participatory Budgeting in Chicago

Ellen Knutson (2014) explored ordinary citizen involvement in Participatory Budgeting (PB) in the 49th Ward of Chicago. While only a small number of citizens in this large city have been given the opportunity to decide a fraction of the city's budget, PB provides them with democratic practice in public decision-making and the chance to make a difference in their neighborhood. Knutson describes the process as follows:

> Alderman Joe Moore was the first US-based elected official to experiment with Participatory Budgeting. In 2010 he gave decision-making power over his discretionary budget to the residents of Chicago's 49th Ward to fund capital improvements in the ward. The PB49 process includes a series of neighborhood assemblies . . . where residents could learn about the PB process and discuss their ideas for what infrastructure projects are needed in the ward. These ideas, generated by the community, are then developed by volunteer community members or budget delegates into project proposals and then prepared for the ballot. On election day and at early voting sites residents of the 49th Ward who are at least 16 years old select their preferred infrastructure projects. You do not have to be a registered voter or even a citizen of the US. Alderman Moore agrees to make the vote binding and implement the top vote getters on the ballot.
>
> The experience of PB does build civic capacity within the residents as well as shows elements of democratic practices. The primary sites for naming and framing are in the neighborhood assemblies. The primary sites for deliberation and identifying resources are in the leadership committee and working committees, with more informal deliberation happening at the assemblies and around the election. There are indicators of acting and learning in the committees especially when one looks across the years. Additionally, PB49 shows evidence of creative problem solving with citizens, businesses and government agencies. Through PB people are able to speak up for what they believe is needed and see it through the implementation process.
>
> The PB process helps educate what can and cannot be done on the ward level. This education and getting a better sense of how city politics work—what can and cannot be accomplished through the Alderman's office—building trust in

> the community and giving ordinary people the power to make decisions changes people's impression of what they can affect on the city level. PB also opens up some avenues for other ways to meet the community's needs.
>
> There are of course some challenges that face PB in the 49th Ward. One that came up in several of the interviews was the notion of setting wardwide priorities, and long-term planning. . . . A second challenge is the lack of multi-year planning for infrastructure.
>
> Of course, priorities are not without contention for residents within the ward, and these tensions sometimes fall along ethnic and class-lines. . . . Working with the community is very labor intensive and face to face meetings are very important . . .a perpetual and labor-intensive activity, but one that was integral to the overall success and health of any PB process. . . . The constraints of menu money is another challenge that PB49 faces. . . . These funds can only be used for capital improvements in the ward and this creates a potential mismatch between community priorities and the dictates of what menu money can fund. . . . Furthermore, there is tension between the PB process and the way city officials and departments typically work. . . . PB does not go by the book and bureaucrats in the systems take some convincing which can impede the implementation of projects that have won the vote.

In short, citizens in the 49th Ward availed themselves of the opportunity to exercise some democratic practices on a small scale through participatory budgeting. The study provided a microscopic view of how citizens may engage with institutions to coproduce public goods. It also demonstrated that some public servants do value input from citizens and see citizens as meaningful contributors in the work of government.

In this case, of course, it was the alderman who possessed power and chose to share it with citizens in his ward. The only levers of power that citizens had were voting and collective action. Citizens were woefully unmatched when engaging city government and major nonprofits no matter how complementary their relations. The big question is: How can the balance of power be shifted in favor of citizens? Nevertheless, PB may be an important civic exercise in giving citizens real opportunities to exercise democratic practices and make a difference in their communities.

PUBLIC PARTICIPATION IN INTERNATIONAL SETTINGS

The last two reports of this section by Jacky Zvulun and Hannah Tsadik add an international perspective through cases from New Zealand and Ethiopia. These cases illuminated the potentially universal nature of democratic practices. The evaluation of these reports paid special attention to the democratic practices that may denote levels of citizen engagement. Researchers were exploring the extent to which citizens were engaging institutions.

Voting in New Zealand

This report explored voter turnout, media coverage, civic education, and types of voting in New Zealand. Jacky Zvulun (2010) examined several electoral systems (Single Transferable Vote and First Past the Post) and voting practices (postal and electronic) as well as media coverage to determine their effects on declining voter turnout. For the most part, he found that these variables did not significantly affect overall voter turnout. There were also conflicting reports on whether civic education alone could increase or improve voter turnout. However, the educated class benefited most by the voting methods as they were most likely to vote in the first place. The author reports on his findings below:

> Participation in elections is a significant exercise in democracy for both citizens and their representatives. . . . Low voter turnout can be seen as evidence of a disengaged, fragmented and unequal society. Recently, democratic countries have witnessed a decline in voting numbers. This phenomenon, which this paper labels as "participation panic," has raised questions about the reasons for the reluctance to vote and the implications of such reluctance for the future. At a local level, citizens may have a better chance of engaging with democracy; voting locally may advance their political skills and may reinforce wider aspects of democracy, including participation at [the] national level, yet, at a local level, generally speaking, turnout has tended to decline further than at a national level. In New Zealand the discussion around low voter turnout at the local level has not generated significant debate. . . . This study is seeking to fill that gap by examining local electoral participation in New Zealand.
>
> The paper evaluates factors that can influence voter turnout, especially the impact of civic education, and the role of electoral administration. For example, postal voting sometimes is seen as one way of increasing voter turnout, yet in this case where postal voting was used, voting returns declined over time. Another way of improving voter turnout is thought to be through electronic voting. However, e-voting was found to have only slight impact on voter turnout. Electoral systems can also have an impact on voter turnout, with proportional representation thought to increase voter turnout. Two different electoral systems were used by different councils in the 2004 New Zealand local elections: Single Transferable Vote (STV) and First Past the Post (FPTP). . . . Finally, this paper looks at the coverage [by] the news media and in particular the print media. . . . The role of the print media in influencing voter turnout between the 2004 and

> 2007 local elections will be discussed with particular reference to information disseminated to the public through newspapers.
>
> New Zealand fitted the general model and is a clear example that [in] local elections voter turnout is lower than [in] national elections. The average voter turnout in [New Zealand] national elections is 80 percent, but in local elections it falls to around 45 percent.
>
> There are two main approaches to explaining trends in voter turnout: via institutional factors or individual-level behavior. Institutional factors concern the way elections are conducted. For example, automatic registration makes voting easier than self-registration. Voting on Saturday or Sunday can be more convenient than voting on a weekday; having more polling booths helps, while postal voting makes voting easier for voters who are further from polling booths or are disabled or ill (Rose 2004). Electoral systems such as proportional representation, civic education, compulsory voting and concurrent elections, may make voting more attractive. Institutions such as the media can also motivate people to vote. (Cook 2005; Silverblatt 2004)

Although voting is an important factor in democratic governance and perhaps the most popular form of political participation, it does not indicate whether citizens have exercised deliberative democratic practices. Not surprisingly, voting does demonstrate that citizens have made political choices whether informed or not. What we may conclude is that New Zealanders vote at a high rate in national elections but not so much in local elections. Whether this means anything important is unknown. However, more important, we can infer that if New Zealanders are predisposed to voting then they may also be likely to exercise other democratic practices.

Small Civic Space in Ethiopia

In this research project, Hannah Tsadik (2015) explores restricted civil society space in Ethiopia, which instituted a civil society law in 2009—the Charities and Societies Proclamation (CSP)—that severely limited large parts of civil society from engaging in specific political activities. She discovers, however, that even in a very repressive political environment creative NGOs or other civil society organizations can work to bring about social change. She explains her research in the passages below:

> The Peace and Development Center (PDC), formally established in 1992, is a non-governmental, nonpartisan and nonprofit organization that grew out of the Ad-Hoc Peace Committee (AHPC). PDC is known to be the first peace NGO founded and run by Ethiopian citizens and diaspora.
>
> Interviewees for this study were unanimous in [stating] that it has been the government that names and frames the problem of conflicts in the Ethiopian

context, especially in the post-2005 election period when a battery of laws were enshrined in 2008–2011 that firmly regulated the activities of media, political parties, and civil society. . . . Beyond defining the problem "naming and framing" also happens at the level of defining who can partake in addressing a particular challenge. The government of Ethiopia sees that it is primarily the government's role to engage in peace and conflict work.

[The Ethiopian Ministry of Justice] argues that the Ethiopian constitution does not afford either foreigners or Ethiopian citizens who operate with foreign funding the right to freedom of association—the fundamental freedom that underpins civil society work—as a matter of right in Ethiopia; it is to be seen as a privilege that the government may grant based on its good-will. As such, organizations formed by non-citizens or citizens funded from abroad may not engage in "political"/advocacy activities as the latter[are] reserved for citizens only. . . . PDC has been able to negotiate a framing with the government that allows for a broader understanding of "who" can engage. . . . However, PDC has yet to sit at the table to be a part of the overarching naming and framing of the problem of peace and conflict.

Once the CSP was promulgated, the vast majority of civil society organizations who worked in peacebuilding opted . . . to exit peace work altogether either by disbanding their organizations or turning to less sensitive areas of engagement around service delivery in health, agriculture, and education. . . . PDC had unique means to embark on a proactive strategy because of its access and standing vis-à-vis the Ethiopian government that allowed the organization to have direct, bilateral negotiations with government on how to accommodate PDC in the new legal dispensation for civil society. . . .A large part of PDC's ability to transcend the restrictions that other civil society organizations faced can be attributed to the fact that the organization's value base and subsequent conduct was grounded in Ethiopian traditions of eldership. . . . As long as a civil society organization is able to mobilize resources from within the country—or operate without it on a voluntary basis—it is free to organize and engage in any manner or area it wishes as long as it does not contravene the 1995 Ethiopian constitution.

The CSP that was seen with "doom and gloom" has brought about unconventional collaboration between civil society and religious organizations, universities and government. . . . The environment created by the CSP has also affirmed Ethiopian traditions as a powerful tool. It has proven that the trust building, relationship building and patience as virtues in civic life stand the test of time.

In sum, the report does not demonstrate how ordinary citizens engage in public life. From what one can surmise, ordinary citizens were not effectively engaged in political life in ways that affect their common future. It appeared that the elders who had standing in their communities were the ones exercising limited democratic practices. The shortfall was that naming and framing problems and issues were largely done by government. Even the elders were left out of this process. The Peace and Development Center (PDC), which has a history of public engagement, primarily through the elders, was the organization that was making a small difference in public life. The elders had political and social capital that were used to navigate the CSP. This proclamation limited the scope and activities of NGOs and citizens in Ethiopia since 2009.

This report revealed that, although Ethiopia has established a democratic form of government, it places severe restrictions on how citizens and NGOs can operate in civil society. Generally speaking, the elders, with special permission, can engage in democratic practices but cannot receive funding from foreign sources; doing so may jeopardize their welfare and safety. However, any NGO that utilizes resources found solely within the country may organize and operate in accordance to the 1995 Constitution and the CSP. All citizens and civil society organizations were prohibited from receiving foreign funding.

Chapter 5 illustrates how democratic citizens in a particular neighborhood name and frame problems and issues without outside control or interference. The Arlington Park neighborhood is an example of what I call a "self-starting and self-sustaining community." This is a community that utilizes its own assets to solve public problems before seeking help from the outside. The community relies on its own skills, abilities, and resources in confronting the challenges facing their community.

Chapter 5

Arlington Park Neighborhood

INTRODUCTION

This chapter documents one neighborhood's efforts to fight and eradicate the incidence of illegal drugs and prostitution activities in a historic district in the largest metropolitan area in Alabama. It is a qualitative study on suspected illegal drugs and prostitution activities in the City of Birmingham located in Jefferson County. Comments by neighbors living in the Arlington Park Historic District, and interviews with the chief of police, City of Birmingham; sheriff, Jefferson County; presiding judge, Criminal Division of District Court, Jefferson County; president, Arlington West End Neighborhood Association; and minutes from the Arlington Park Neighborhood Association (the author served as president of this association) constitute the data for the study. A group of citizens that make up the association of property owners in Arlington Park Neighborhood have committed themselves to address the suspected illegal drugs and prostitution problems in their community. This group petitioned city officials to form a task force for the expressed purpose of eliminating the incidence of illegal drugs and prostitution activities in Arlington Park Historic District.

The Arlington Park Neighborhood is a part of the larger West End community located in Birmingham, Alabama. Arlington Park was added to the National Register of Historic Places in 1995. This designation was based on the district's architectural and historical significance to the area. In a 1994 historical survey, sixty-eight residences of the neighborhood were listed as contributing historical resources (Arlington West End Neighborhood Improvement Plan 2002). West End, a portion of which was formerly known as Elyton, has been populated since the early 1800s, even before Alabama joined the United States. Elyton preexisted the founding of Birmingham and was incorporated in 1821 and served as the first permanent county seat of Jefferson County (Arlington West End Neighborhood Improvement Plan 2002).

In 1865, Gen. James H. Wilson (Union Army) "left Jasper (Alabama) with the rest of the troops after daylight on March 30 and arrived in Elyton at One O'clock in the afternoon. He ate lunch at Judge William S. Mudd's house, 'The Grove' (now Arlington)" (Rogers et al. 1994, 220). In 1871, Birmingham was incorporated in an old cornfield 3 miles east of Elyton. Arlington Park is the centerpiece of this historic community and grew around the Arlington House that dates back to 1850 (Arlington West End Neighborhood Improvement Plan 2002).

Neighbors living in the Arlington Park Historic District noticed an increase in suspected illegal drug and prostitution activities in apartments and houses on Cotton Avenue Southwest, Center Street, Lomb Avenue Southwest, and Tuscaloosa Avenue Southwest. Neighbors reported to law enforcement and city officials a number of suspicious individuals and automobiles frequently seen at or near suspected drug houses and apartments and/or cruising and parking in the general vicinity. Residents reported an increased flow of suspicious automobiles and individuals stopping and passing through the historic neighborhood of Arlington Park. Neighbors reported cars parked on streets and at apartments with hoods and trunks up and doors opened with suspicious individuals tinkering about or standing nearby. Residents also observed increased emergency calls to the area related to crime or suspected criminal activity.

In addition, neighbors reported ladies walking the bordering streets in the Arlington Park neighborhood flagging down and entering the cars of strangers in what appeared to be prostitution activities. Drug paraphernalia and female undergarments were found at the scene of some of these suspicious activities. Residents observed suspicious-looking individuals carrying book bags; using cell phones; and walking through the neighborhood, entering suspected drug houses, apartments, and automobiles; and interacting with other suspected individuals or otherwise loitering at suspected locations. Neighbors witnessed this cycle of suspicious activity on a daily basis for several years. The increasing incidence of suspected illegal drug and prostitution activities became a major concern of neighbors in Arlington Park and motivated the property owners in the historic district to petition city officials to form a special task force to address the matter.

FRAMING THE ISSUE IN PUBLIC TERMS

Neighbors of Arlington Park reported at a meeting that the increasing crime and illegal drugs in the neighborhood and surrounding apartments contributed to prostitution, theft, and other drug-related activities. The apartment complex was a major concern and eyesore for residents. Residents expressed concern over theft of property, prostitution, shootings, drug use and sales, and abandoned houses in the immediate area (Arlington Park Neighborhood Minutes, November 23, 2003). Several suggestions were made to attack the problems identified above. One suggestion was to solicit the help of Channel 13 (NBC affiliate)—*The Investigator*—to highlight the problem the neighborhood was experiencing as a news documentary report. Another suggestion was to attend a city council meeting and appeal for help. Neighbors were asked to fill out incident reports for all occurrences of criminal behavior witnessed in the neighborhood (Arlington Park Neighborhood Minutes, November 23, 2003).

Residents framed eight community issues as targets for aggressive community action in 2004. One of which was framed as "criminal activity overflows into neighborhood" (Arlington Park Neighborhood Minutes, January 11, 2004).

1. *Street lights out at intersections and entrance into the historic district are deplorable.*
   Street lights are out at the intersections of Cotton and Center Street, and Cotton and Lomb. They have been out more than one and one-half years. This situation is dangerous at night and during the winter months when it gets dark early. Also, as the only Antebellum Home in the city, where visitors from all over the world visit annually, the entrances to the Arlington House and the Arlington Park Neighborhood are deplorable. From downtown, First Avenue North leading up to the Arlington Park Neighborhood, the roadway is riddled with trash, debris, and dilapidated structures, buildings, and houses. This is not the image that Birmingham wants to project, nor what visitors from around the country and world need to see when visiting the historic Arlington House.
2. *Criminal activity overflows into neighborhood.* Criminal activity, including illegal drugs and prostitution, overflows into the neighborhood. These illegal activities have encroached our neighborhood as a result of several problems in the apartment buildings located on Cotton Avenue, Center Street, and at Loveman Village, and outsiders coming into the neighborhood to buy and sell drugs; despite residents constantly calling 311 about such problems, these activities continue.
3. *Vacant/abandoned houses.* Abandoned, vacant, and dilapidated houses, including the Montgomery Cottage, devalue the historical integrity of the neighborhood. Condemnation is warranted in some cases.
4. *Inadequate storm sewer and drainage system.* The storm sewer and drainage system is problematic on Munger Avenue, First Street, and

Second Street SW. The ditch on Second Street causes water to stand, which incubates mosquitoes.

5. *Pavement of sidewalks and streets.* The streets and sidewalks need repaving in the neighborhood on First, Second, Third, and Fourth Streets, Munger, McMillon, and Cotton Avenues. The neighborhood's streets and sidewalks have not been repaved in more than 20 years.
6. *Promised second phase of street lanterns were never installed.* The neighborhood was promised that street lanterns would be installed throughout the historic district. That promise was made more than 10 years ago. To date, the promise has not been kept.
7. *Lack of enforcement of basketball and leash laws.* Because there is a lack of enforcement of basketball and leash laws (even when calls are made to 311 reporting violations), young children, the elderly, and community members in general are at risk of being injured and/or maimed.
8. *Street vendors.* Street vendors on the corner of First Avenue North and Center Street create a nuisance and devalue the properties of the community.

Crimes reported by neighbors included car burglary, a backyard prowler, auto vandalism, theft of CDs, and a garage break-in (Arlington Park Neighborhood Minutes, February 15, 2004). City Councilor stated that she would "propose an increase in police patrol and speak with the Chief of Police about more crime prevention." The councilor would also look at the possibility of CAP officers (bike patrol) patrolling the neighborhood. She also would ask for a task force for Arlington (Arlington Park Neighborhood Minutes, February 15, 2004).

In an interview the sheriff asserted, "If you look at deputies per thousands, we fall 114 deputies short" (Sheriff Interview, January 27, 2005). Birmingham police officers are not up to strength either. Perhaps, that may partially explain some of the crime activity. A thief opened the back door of a storage shed and stole some items. A neighbor's car window was broken and another's SUV was broken into, and another neighbor's car was stolen as he watched the thief (Arlington Park Neighborhood Minutes, March 21, 2004).

Some criminals were apprehended as a result of one neighbor reporting tag numbers. The Drug Task Force also was notified. A police officer stated that the police department needed a track record of all incidents so that they could build a file (Arlington Park Neighborhood Minutes, April 18, 2004). University of Alabama at Birmingham Treatment Alternatives to Street Crimes (UAB TASC) received a grant for a program called Drug Usage Forecasting (DUF) to drug test city and county jail inmates to determine what impact illegal drug use and illegal drugs were having on crime. According to the presiding judge, "Anywhere from 68 to 74 percent of the people who went to jail charged from murder to shoplifting was 'dirty' with illegal drugs at the time of arrest. The urine tested positive. Cocaine was prominent and marijuana was pretty strong" (Presiding Judge Interview, January 26, 2005). A fire at the apartments was the results of tenants freebasing. One tenant died. The city's legal department was working on the apartments. There was one raid. One of the neighbors reported that prostitutes might have moved to the area by the Arlington Cleaners (Arlington Park Neighborhood Minutes, April 18, 2004). Two suspected con artists approached a neighbor claiming an emergency. They asked for a cup of water but fled when they saw his spouse drive up to the house. They stole a weed eater. A medical kit was stolen from a neighbor's car. A person described as tall and wearing a big Afro was seen burglarizing a neighbor's car. Suspicious and strange-looking characters have been seen in the neighborhood (Arlington Park Neighborhood Minutes, June 20, 2004).

Several residents attended a Nuisance Hearing at the County Courthouse concerning the apartments on Tuscaloosa Avenue. The judge was impressed by the turnout of eleven neighbors from the Arlington Park Neighborhood. Under the Drug Nuisance and Abatement Act, the judge ordered the owner of the troubled apartments (not the ones closest to the historic district) in the area to hire twenty-four-hour security for a period of time and report back to the court. The security guard at the Arlington House alerted a neighbor that a suspected drug dealer driving a white panel truck/van was in the neighborhood. A water fountain and generator were stolen from a neighbor's yard (Arlington Park Neighborhood Minutes, August 15, 2004).

The apartments on Cotton Avenue were raided twice. Police were monitoring the neighborhood. It was recommended that neighbors refrain from confronting suspected drug dealers. A blue Caprice station wagon and a white van had been seen speeding through the neighborhood. A red car was in contact with the van passenger who drove through to complete a drug transaction. The "dealer" lives in the neighborhood. A brown UPS truck and a car had been observed parked across from the Arlington House. Prostitutes at the apartment complex were under surveillance. A neighbor suggested that a request be made to Chief of Police for more frequent drive-through by police (Arlington Park Neighborhood Minutes, September 19, 2004). "Drugs and narcotics are part of most every crime. For example, the 'meth' (methamphetamine) labs—when they are not cooking the 'meth'—when they weren't selling these drugs they had their addicts going through mailboxes stealing credit card numbers and credit cards" (Sheriff Interview2005).

> "Drug addicts are young and old, black and white, rich and poor. We got a lot of them who get caught with forced prescriptions. Or they get caught with drugs on a traffic stop. They aren't committing crimes to support a drug habit. They

> can afford to buy the drugs. . . . I see a lot of middle-class, middle-age, white females in Drug Court—school teachers, housewives, businesswomen who get hooked on a drug called lortab, which is hydrocodone. They steal a prescription pad and write their own prescription."
>
> (Presiding Judge Interview, January 26, 2005)

In sum, these seemingly persistent and illegal acts occurring in and around the Arlington Park Historic District formed the impetus for public outcry and action. Therefore, a strategy was adopted to mobilize and activate resources to effectively eradicate the problem of illegal drug and prostitution activities in the district. The Arlington Park Neighborhood is within the core of the inner city and experiences all of the problems and challenges typically associated with postmodern urban environments, such as high incidences of crime and crime-related activities. Over the last five years, there has been an increase in calls to police, fire, and rescue personnel to attend to residents in nearby apartment complexes and suspected drug houses. There has been an increase in burglaries, vandalism, transients, and vagrants wandering through the neighborhood. Concomitantly, there has been a rise in the number and frequency of ladies strolling the streets, flagging down strangers, and entering the automobiles of suspected "Joes" and returning back to the community to repeat the cycle. The rapid-fire sound of automatic gunfire has also increased in frequency and proximity to the neighborhood.

In short, property owners of the Arlington Park Neighborhood have witnessed these suspicious activities, considered them to be of grave concern, and delivered a clarion call to public officials to act with all available means at their disposal to eliminate illegal drugs and prostitution activities in the historic district. The property owners of Arlington Park formerly requested the City of Birmingham to form a task force to eradicate (root and branch) the infestation of illegal drug and prostitution activities from the Arlington Park community.

GOVERNMENT'S RESPONSE

Below are brief descriptors of the responses of government officials and others to the eight community issues:

- Increased visibility of marked and unmarked law enforcement personnel in the area.
- FBI, DEA, and local law enforcement personnel attendance at neighborhood meetings.

- The mayor, city councilor, city attorney, and county commissioner attended neighborhood meetings.
- Public officials surveyed the area and identified issues to address.
- The Police Chief, Sheriff, Drug Court Judge, and neighborhood president (agent of city government) granted interviews for the study.
- The Arlington Park Neighborhood appeared before the city council twice to address the identified issues that resulted in a tour of the historic district by public officials, news media, and neighborhood officers.

RESULTS

The results of government response and citizen engagement are indicated below:

- Increased law enforcement presence for a period of time.
- Patched two potholes.
- Razed two abandoned houses.
- Conducted two drug raids with arrests.
- Court-ordered twenty-four-hour security for troubled apartments. However, these troubled apartments were not the ones across the street from the historic district.
- Increased awareness of neighborhood issues in the Birmingham area.
- Set roadblocks in the area as a tactic to curtail criminal activity.
- Used decoys to bait and arrest solicitors of prostitution.

BEST PRACTICES

The following list includes things that may be considered best practices that would better serve public administrators and law enforcement officials in attacking the problems identified by the Arlington Park Neighborhood.

- Implement a game plan around crime statistics on the area.
- Prioritize and target-specific drug-related crime and prostitution activities in the area.
- Form a task force that would be visible in fighting crime in the area.
- Conduct more frequent raids and busts.
- Place the entire historic district under surveillance. It is only six blocks.
- Implement community policing in the area.
- Crackdown on vagrancy.
- Setup a police substation in the immediate area.

SUMMARY

In the Arlington Park Neighborhood case, government failed to eradicate the systemic problems of crime against property, illegal drugs, and prostitution activities. Some reasons for failure: (1) Both the Police Chief and the Sheriff argued the need for more law enforcement personnel. They claimed that their forces were understaffed. They cited budget cuts and attrition rates (officers retiring or being recruited by suburban municipalities). In addition, they asserted (2) inability to recruit and train fast enough to keep up, and (3) politics-as-usual: the squeaky wheel gets the oil. NIMBY—some politicians act as though if it is not in my backyard or my strongest supporters' backyards, it is not a problem or priority. Therefore, they offered "lip service" to quail complaints and protests. (4) Some individuals might have been career or professional criminals. Law enforcement personnel argued that crime is an avocation for some people. This is how they make a living by burglarizing homes, selling drugs, and selling their bodies. They use these methods to support their habits and families. The pay is good and they become immune to law enforcement and the court system. (5) Criminals are crafty in the sense that they know how to stay one step ahead of law enforcement. By habit, they have become accustomed to the legal system and in many ways have become adept at manipulating the system. They have "lawyered up" and found all of the loopholes in the system, which may explain why some prostitutes are repeatedly arrested and released; and the same for some drug users and dealers. Some criminals also use threat and intimidation tactics through their dress and behavior. The wearing of sagging pants by people considered "thugs" and "gang bangers" exposing undergarments, flashing guns, and driving "pimped out" automobiles are all symbols of crime and violence. The bottom-line is that government may be too big and cumbersome, similar to the U.S. military and the war on terrorism, to adjust on the ground to effectively defeat small unconventional targets or operations. (6) Institutional collapse—the church, school, family, and the legal system have failed as a group of people who comprise the criminal class has become bold and sophisticated over time.

These social systems have created a class of people as a byproduct who have little respect for themselves or others. This lawless underclass operates in a subculture to eke out in most cases a standard of living by illegal means that they otherwise could not afford. Punishment is not a deterrent as this class of social deviants abides by its own rules. Thus, one of America's largest cities needs to develop better methods and tactics for eradicating crime, illegal drugs, and prostitution activities.

However, the property owners in the Arlington Park Neighborhood were heard by city and county public officials. These public officials attended neighborhood meetings, provided information and advice, allocated resources, and made promises to continue monitoring the situation. City officials worked on the list of problems with some success. Overall, the citizens of the Arlington Park Neighborhood exercised a measure of control over their common future.

The case of Arlington Park, however, may be atypical because a significant number of property owners had meaningful associations with public officials and administrators on state and local levels. These reciprocal relationships opened doors and provided access to power structures unavailable to ordinary citizens in many communities. In other words, these property owners exercised social and political capital that enabled them to garner attention and obtain resources necessary to address their public problems.

Chapter 6 explores the most popular form of citizen participation—public hearing—through the case of the New Jersey Turnpike Authority. This chapter illuminates how the Authority operates and achieves its public participation goals. The chapter reveals how the participation process is controlled by the Authority from agenda setting to policy implementation.

Chapter 6

A Case Study of New Jersey's 2008 Toll Policy Decision

INTRODUCTION

In 2008, the New Jersey Turnpike Authority (NJTA) proposed roadway toll rate increases to meet its debt service obligations and for capital improvements, which included constructing a third tunnel between New Jersey and New York. In this case, citizens were invited to participate through public hearings, letter writing, faxing, and e-mailing. An unassuming citizen might deem these mechanisms as effective ways for citizens to participate. However, these activities do not necessarily equate to political equality as this chapter explains effective citizen participation. After the Authority held four public hearings and received public input, the toll increase proposal was adopted. The Authority gained tacit public approval to proceed with its plan.

The significance of the 2008 toll policy on citizens was that its enactment constituted the largest single toll increase in NJTA's history, raising toll fares substantially over time from a low of 10 percent to a high of 50 percent per increase. According to the Authority's own estimates, the "tolls would increase by 50 percent (2009), 50 percent (2012), and 10 percent (2023), respectively, on the Turnpike for both passenger vehicles and commercial trucks" (Notice of Supplemental Public Hearing for a Toll Adjustment 2008, 1). Their estimates indicated that "Tolls would increase by 43% (2009), 50% (2012) and 10% (2023) in that order, on the Garden State Parkway for both passenger vehicles and commercial trucks" (1). Conservatively, those rate changes would raise some $10 billion within ten years.

Should citizens engage in toll policymaking? In a democracy, whether direct, representative, or otherwise, the authority of government belongs to the people. Public officials are elected or appointed to represent the authority on behalf of citizens. President Lincoln asserted that basic principle of democracy in his historic Gettysburg Address that government was "of the people, by the people, and for the people" (Bruun and Crosby 1999, 425). If government were not as Lincoln suggested, then public administrators, elected officials, and experts would be free to impose their will on the people. The Antifederalists, as represented by Smith (as cited in Ketcham 2003), argued that "the nearer the representative is to his constituent, the more attached and dependent he will be" (Ketcham 2003, 355). In that case, the representative would be instructed regarding the wishes of the people and held accountable for his actions. Madison, a Federalist, stated in Federalist #51 "If men were angels no government would be necessary. If angels were to govern men, neither external or internal controls would be necessary" (Madison 2003, 317). History is replete with examples that men are not angels, and angels do not govern them either.

Citizens traveling along and through New Jersey via the New Jersey Turnpike, the Garden State Parkway, and the Atlantic City Express inadvertently invested in the NJTA each time they paid a fare when passing through a toll plaza as motor vehicle operators. By making an involuntary investment—which came directly from their pocketbooks—citizens gained a vested interest in the toll policy additional to their common interest and, thus, earned an extra privilege to have a voice in the policymaking process whether they exercised that privilege or not. Accordingly, citizens were provided the privilege to voice concerns or offer feedback to policymakers or not, at least at the formulation stage, through one or more of seven possible avenues: (a) accept the proposal, (b) attend a public hearing, (c) participate during the public comment period, (d) utilize the appeal process, (e) engage in a public protest, (f) litigate, or (g) decline direct involvement. Having a voice in the policymaking process, however, did not grant citizens the ability to set toll rates or enable them to have direct influence on the toll rate structure. They did not get to determine when rate changes would take effect or decide the frequency at which rate changes would occur. Ultimately, citizens were left to cope with subsequent toll policy changes and the unintended consequences of those changes regardless of their level of involvement in the policymaking process.

Some of the unintended consequences the toll policy initiative had on motorists who routinely traveled New Jersey toll highways included inconveniences that cost citizens more time and money and adversely affected the quality of their daily lives: loss of time due to resorting to inconvenient routes or secondary and tertiary roads to avoid paying tolls, travel time disrupted by congested roads in neighborhoods; additional noise and air pollution generated by queuing at tolling plazas or idling at traffic lights; and an increase in fuel consumption due to extended travel routes. Citizens were forced to make decisions regarding whether to travel a toll road or free road (if available) to get from point A to point B. Since public officials had made toll roads the most convenient and direct routes, citizens were manipulated into paying the toll fare even if it constituted a hardship or if it were against their will. Surprisingly, New Jersey had created a toll triangle with bordering states New York and Pennsylvania. The axis points connected Atlantic City, New York City, and Philadelphia. Motorists paid the toll whether going to work, traveling leisurely, attending to an emergency, or running an errand.

In an ideal republican form of government, citizens have authority to influence policy and hold public officials accountable. However, not in the Garden State, citizens in New Jersey did not appear to control or effectively influence toll policy. That power was granted to the Authority by law (New Jersey Turnpike Authority 2004). The Authority's only responsibilities to citizens were to inform them forty-five days in advance of the effective date of a rate change, to hold a public hearing, to make certain information public, and to allow for petition to address a policy concern (New Jersey Turnpike Authority 2004). What was problematic about this arrangement was that a forty-five-day period might not have been an enough time for citizens to become informed on the proposal, to consider policy options, or to learn about all of the policy's unintended consequences. Such a short notice may not have given citizens or citizen-groups sufficient time to become educated or to organize and acquire resources to mount an effective opposition to the policy if they deem it necessary.

For more than fifty years, interest groups had lobbied public officials and influenced public policy in New Jersey. More than 1,000 registered lobbyists, serving some 1,500 clients, were in existence in Trenton in 2007 (Salmoreand Salmore 2008, 110). That number grew exponentially as compared with the twenty that McKean identified in the 1930s, the seventy who registered in 1964 when it was first required, and the 254 who registered in 1976 (Salmore and Salmore 2008, 110). As perceived by their effectiveness and high credibility rating, the New Jersey Education Association and the New Jersey Business and Industry Association were considered the most influential and effective interest groups in the state (Salmore and Salmore 2008, 113).

Based on the number of registered lobbyists in New Jersey, special interests, especially business and education, were well represented. Assuming that the public's interest was not necessarily the same as that of business and education, three questions came to mind: (a) What level of participation did ordinary citizens have in the policymaking process? (b) How effective were citizens' influence on public policy matters? (c) What mechanisms were utilized to include citizens in the public policy process? I addressed these questions as they related to roadway toll policymaking in the state in 2008. The New Jersey State Legislature established provisions for giving citizens a voice in such matters through statewide referenda. However, citizens were permitted by the NJTA to participate in public hearings and to communicate their concerns by fax, mail, and e-mail only.

The problem was positioned in the Authority relying on public hearings as its primary mechanism for engaging citizens in policymaking. Public hearings were not effective mechanisms for engaging the public because: they were often inconsequential; they permitted sanctioned-isolation; and they allowed for agency control (Cole and Caputo 1984; King et al. 1998). Public hearings tended to be perfunctory activities that public authorities and governmental agencies could utilize to sway public opinion or otherwise to impose their will upon the public.

New Jersey Turnpike Authority

Governor Driscoll was considered the father of the New Jersey Turnpike Authority (Salmore and Salmore 2008, 345). During his 1947 inaugural address, he called for the construction of the New Jersey Turnpike. According to Salmore and Salmore, "quiet conversations about the patronage possibilities inherent in $250 million worth of equipment contracts, construction jobs, and a small army of toll collectors helped Driscoll win legislative assent for a Turnpike Authority in 1948" (Salmore and Salmore 2008, 345). Three years later the 118-mile superhighway opened in 1951. It was followed by other toll roads namely the Garden State Parkway in 1955 and the Atlantic City Expressway in 1964 (Salmore and Salmore 2008, 345).

In 2008, the New Jersey Turnpike spanned 148 miles and ran primarily north and south on the west side of the state, connected eastward to Interstate 95 near the Hudson River, and moved westward and southward down to the Delaware River. According to Stansfield, it was one of the most heavily traveled thorough fares in the United States, at more than 200 million vehicles per year (Stansfield 2004, 173). In 2003, the legislature authorized combining the Garden State Parkway with the Turnpike Authority. The Parkway ran north and south from Bergen County to Cape May County, spanning 173 miles (primarily along the east side of the state). Together, the New Jersey Turnpike, the New Jersey Garden State Parkway, and the Atlantic City Expressway encompassed 19 percent of New Jersey's traffic and 321 miles of the state's highway system.

The Authority collected $856,457,039 revenue with net revenue of $92,021,827 in the fiscal year 2008 and $863,270,638 revenue with net revenue of $94,556,203 in 2007 (Audited Financial Statements 2008). The NJTA, comprising eight appointed officials (seven commissioners plus the director of the New Jersey Department of Transportation), was a government-sponsored monopoly that had exclusive rights to construct and manage toll facilities, including setting the toll rate schedules within the state. Established in 1948, the NJTA grew into the state's all-powerful public utility. New Jersey law, as amended, stated, "There is hereby established in the State Department of Transportation a body corporate and politic, with corporate succession, to be known as the New Jersey Turnpike Authority, Section 3 of P.L. 1948, c. 454 (C.27: 23-3), subsection 3 (A)." That aspect of the law indicated that the NJTA operated like a business, where commissioners set policy, determined the fee structure, and employees managed daily operations.

PROBLEM STATEMENT

Ordinary citizens were at the mercy of commissioners and management and were subject to fines and jail sentences for violation of adopted toll policies. The financial impact on daily toll road commuters was consequential, and in some cases punitive (Section 10 of P.L. 1951, c. 264, C.27: 23-34). Citizens appeared to have had very little influence, if any, on the Authority. Yet, they experienced the burden of the Authority's decisions and actions, including unintended consequences. In accordance to the law, the Authority could have changed rate structures any time and for any reason it chose. Section 1 of P.L. 1977, c. 230 (C.27: 23-5.10), as amended, stated the Authority, whenever it decides to change policy, must hold a public hearing on a proposal forty-five days before its effective date.

In this case, if the Authority so chose, it could have initiated a toll hike anytime shortfalls in its revenue were projected. A forty-five-day period may not constitute a reasonable or sufficient public notice. Even though it was the responsibility of commissioners to ensure that the Authority met its fiduciary responsibility, such a short period of time limited the ability of citizens to effectively engage in policymaking. Such constraints may not have given ordinary citizens ample time to inform themselves on the need for rate increases.

Section 9 of P.L. 1948, c. 454 (C.27: 23-29), subsection 9 (A), as amended, was liberally constructed, authorizing NJTA to engage in projects other than roads, bridges, and tunnels. Hence, the Authority could divert its attention and resources to the construction, management, or leasing of amusement parks, sports complexes, or casinos, if it deemed necessary. That practice was problematic if the Authority acted irresponsibly, if it were not held accountable, or if citizens were not effectively engaged in its affairs, especially with regards to determining toll policy. Perhaps if the Authority were restricted to projects pertaining only to roads, bridges, and tunnels, there would have been less need to increase toll rates. Ventures such as those cited earlier cost citizens millions of dollars. Consequently, surplus revenue could have been used solely for the maintenance, renovation, and construction of roads, bridges, and tunnels.

Researchers from the last thiry-five years cited public hearing as the most common but ineffective mechanism used to engage citizens in policy decisions. Those researchers revealed that, although citizen participation had been frequently studied during that time period, governments had not fully instituted effective or authentic participation methods (Cole and Caputo 1984). The problem was that government purported to value public input but has not adopted effective means for achieving the same. From 1984, when Cole and Caputo looked at the public hearing process, to 2009, when Woods examined public participation mechanisms, public administration, and communication scholars had studied how and to what extent citizens had been involved in public policymaking. The researchers suggested that citizen participation in the policymaking process had been low to moderate.

This phenomenon continued to elevate the classic tension between the role of the administrative state and that of citizens in deciding public policy. There appeared to be a paradox between government intentions and citizen involvement in public policy. In 1998, King et al. observed that there was a historic contradiction in the U.S. political system regarding the role of citizen participation (King et al. 1998, 318). The tension was located in a desire for public input and a safeguard against too much citizen participation. Attempting to maintain harmony in the administrative state and upholding democratic ideals was like walking a tightrope. There was no consensus in the field as to what constituted effective participation and how it would be measured. Nor were there compelling evidence that governments and agencies that used citizen participation mechanisms considered them worthwhile. Yang and Callahan (2007) found that local governments frequently utilized public participation methods but were less likely to include citizen's input into decision-making (Yang and Callahan 2007, 254).

A few scholars had attempted to state what public participation meant. King et al. argued that authentic participation required deep and continuous involvement in administrative processes with the potential to effect the situation by all involved (King 1998, 320). This statement was consistent with Dahl's (1998) notion of effective participation. Dahl stated that all members must have equal and effective opportunities to make their views known before a policy is decided (Dahl 1998, 37). In 2006, Webler and Tuler described appropriate public participation as a good process that reached out to all stakeholders, shared information openly, engaged people, and satisfied multiple interests (Webler and Tuler 2006, 699). This notion too was consistent with Dahl's (1998) theory regarding political equality.

METHODOLOGY

A qualitative content analysis was used to examine and analyze data from public hearings transcripts, public comments, and other records to ascertain the level and effect of citizen participation on the policy. Dahl's (1998) theory of a democratic process was used. In essence, the process suggested that citizens had both equal and effective opportunities to have their voices heard. Dahl's (1998) democratic process served as the theoretical framework, which guided the two research questions:

(1) To what extent were citizens involved in the policy decision?
(2) What effect did citizens' participation have on the final toll policy decision?

Recorded text from testimonies made in four transcribed public hearings as well as all letters of support and opposition, ranging from traditional letters to e-mails and faxes, were examined and assigned codes. Special notations were given to each piece of evidence depending on whether testimony denoted opposition to, support for, or undecided about the proposed measure.

The data for the New Jersey study included public comments, transcripts, and documents arising from public hearings, meetings, and the public comment period of the NJTA, along with the Authority's response to them. These data represented opinions and expressions from individuals, corporations, businesses, governments, groups, and organizations. The Authority collected and compiled these documents for public record. More than 2,300 pieces of data were reviewed, codified, and analyzed to answer stated research questions. A systematic analysis of the proposals, transcripts, public comments, and records revealed the level and effect of citizen participation on the New Jersey 2008 toll policy decision.

There was an examination of the initial toll increase proposal and the revised version of the proposal (the final adopted proposal) to reveal changes and differences. Differences between the initial proposal and the revised proposal revealed the extent of the citizens' effect on the initiative.

Theoretical Framework

Dahl's (1998) theory of democratic process provided criteria for assessing democratic practices in a state. His theory included five basic tenets: effective participation, equality in voting, enlightened understanding, final control over the agenda, and inclusion of all or most adults.

In explaining the five criteria for a democratic process, Dahl described the first criterion as effective participation stating that, all members must have equal and effective involvement in sharing their views on a policy proposal before it is adopted (Dahl 1998, 37). All members of the association were politically equal and their voices carried equal weight. Their opinions counted on matters of importance. According to Dahl, if some members are given preference over others, adopted policies are likely to reflect their views (Dahl 1998, 39). In other words, a small group of members could control the agenda and set policies in extreme instances (Dahl 1998, 39). For Dahl, the effective participation criterion was designed to cure that effect (Dahl 1998, 39).

Dahl contended that the second basic tenet of a democratic process was voting equality, where every member had an equal and effective vote (Dahl 1998, 37). He reasoned, if all members were qualified to participate, why would not their votes be equal? (Dahl 1998, 39). If this principle were adopted for the 2008 New Jersey toll initiative, then New Jersey citizens would have experienced voting equality. The toll initiative was never offered as a public referendum nor did citizens have a vote on it otherwise.

According to Dahl, the third tenet, enlightened understanding, occurred when all members have equal and effective opportunities to become informed about policy alternatives and consequences. He maintained that enlightened understanding was to ensure that these privileges existed for all members (Dahl 1998, 39). That aspect of a democratic process suggested that citizens were given sufficient notice and had ample opportunities to be informed about policy decisions and their likely consequences. Although Dahl argued that the first three criteria may have seemed sufficient, he reasoned that some members might be opposed to treating all as political equals in governing the affairs of the association. Consequently, what they sought was a provision that would allow them to prevail no matter what a majority of members might adopt in a free and fair vote (Dahl 1998, 40).

The fourth criterion broached the crux of the matter in terms of the public policymaking process. Dahl maintained that control of the agenda was essential in democratic practices because "members must have the exclusive opportunity to decide how and, if they choose, what matters are to be placed on the agenda" (Dahl 1998, 38). Consequently, the democratic process is never closed and can be always changed by membership (Dahl 1998, 38). Dahl reasoned that a small group could control the agenda and never consider proposal alternatives (Dahl 1998, 38). Citizens not having the ability to control of the agenda negated any ability they had to determine public policy. The NJTA's public policymaking process prevented citizens from having the ability to determine what was brought forward as public policy proposals. The process appeared to prohibit effective citizen participation.

Dahl maintained that true democracy provided opportunities for the inclusion of most adults. He postulated that "all, or at any rate most, adult permanent residents should have the full rights of citizenship that are implied by the first four criteria" (Dahl 1998, 38). He argued that giving everyone a voice was not acceptable by most democratic advocates prior to the 1900s (Dahl 1998, 38). According to Dahl those deprived of an equal voice in government will not have their interest represented in a state (Dahl 1998, 76).

FINDINGS

The findings of this case study on NJTA's 2008 toll increase proposals were extrapolated from the data generated, collected, and stored by the Authority. This case study was a qualitative content analysis of the NJTA's records pertaining to the 2008 toll policy initiative. These data were analyzed and evaluated here.

TUNNELS, BRIDGES, TOLL TRIANGLE

There were two tunnels and a network of large bridges between New Jersey and New York. The Holland Tunnel was connected to the Turnpike and channeled non-rail traffic into Lower Manhattan. The Lincoln Tunnel carried rail traffic into Penn Station in Midtown Manhattan. The New Jersey case concerned a proposed second rail tunnel running parallel to the Lincoln Tunnel and delivering rail traffic into Penn Station. The bridges had entry points into and exit points from Upper, Midtown, and Lower Manhattan.

Although not addressed in this chapter, one significant discovery was that New Jersey had created a "toll triangle" with roadway connections between the bordering states of New York and Pennsylvania; the cities of Manhattan, Philadelphia, and Atlantic City serving as axes. Motorists traveling along the perimeter of the triangle and within its confines paid tolls.

The Authority arranged and conducted four public hearings and scheduled a public comment period to generate, collect, and record public input on the proposed toll policy initiative of 2008. These data consisted of public hearing transcripts; e-mail, fax, and mail comments and statements; and the Authority's response. The data were organized and stored at the headquarters of the Authority, under the supervision of its law department.

AUTHORIZATION OF PUBLIC HEARINGS

The Authority was empowered by its Commission initially to conduct three public hearings for the purpose of gaining public input on the proposal (Chairman's document dated October 7, 2008). Corzine, the sitting governor of New Jersey in 2008, proposed a $9.7 billion toll initiative and a $1.25 billion capital investment (raised through tolls) in the Area Regional Core

(ARC) tunnel that would attract another $3 billion from the federal government. The $9.7 billion was earmarked for roadway widening, repair, and maintenance on the Turnpike and Parkway.

In response to public comments and a mandate from the governor, a fourth public hearing was held on October 10, 2008, to solicit public input on the Authority's revised proposal. Those comments were added to the body of data collected and held by the Authority pertaining to the toll policy initiative. The revised proposal included a $2.7 billion reduction in capital projects, retention of the $1.25 billion for the ARC tunnel project, earmarks for the road widening projects and most of the repair projects, and discounts for seniors, commercial vehicles, and low-emission vehicles.

As required by law, before the Authority could effect a change in toll policy, it had to give public notice or hold a public hearing forty-five days in advance. The published timeline for the toll initiative, as shown in table 6.1, covered a thirty-two-day period.

Other than retaining the data for public record, the Authority had no legal obligation to do anything with the public information received from the hearings. The Authority, however, fulfilled its legal duty to make an announcement or hold a hearing or comment period forty-five days in advance of implementation. In essence, the governor appeared to satisfy his primary goal of raising the $1.25 billion for the tunnel project and a secondary goal of roadway widening and maintenance projects.

The Authority held four public hearings for the expressed purpose of taking public comments. Those hearings were not question-and-answer sessions, although officials attempted to answer basic questions.

Public Hearings

The first public hearing was held on Tuesday, September 23, 2008, at Camden County Community College in Blackwood, New Jersey, at 6:00

Table 6.1 New Jersey Toll Initiative Timeline

September 9, 2008	Commission approved scheduling three public hearings
September 11–12, 2008	Authority advertised notice of public hearings in eleven newspapers
September 23, 2008	First public hearing
September 23 to October 2, 2008	Public comment period
September 24, 2008	Second and third public hearings
October 10, 2008	Fourth public hearing and adoption of toll proposal by Authority

Source: NJTA Commission Minutes, Commission Chair Memorandum, 2008.

Table 6.2 Cumulative Total of Speakers at Hearings

Public Hearings	N	*Proponents*	*Opponents*	*Undecided*
First	29	12	7	10
Second	34	20	8	6
Third	24	12	12	0
Fourth	23	5	11	7
Totals	110	49 (45%)	38 (35%)	23 (21%)

Source: NJTA Transcripts of Public Hearings, 2008.

p.m. As table 6.2 indicated, there were twenty-nine speakers recognized and recorded at this hearing.

The second public hearing was held on Wednesday, September 24, 2008, at the NJTA headquarters in Woodbridge, New Jersey, at 9:00 a.m. As table 6.2 indicated, there were thiry-four speakers recognized and recorded at that hearing.

The third public hearing was held on Wednesday, September 24, 2008, at Bergen Community College in Paramus, New Jersey, at 12:20 p.m. As table 6.2 indicated, there were twenty-four speakers recognized and recorded at that hearing.

The fourth and final public hearing was held on Friday, October 10, 2008, at the New Jersey Turnpike Authority in Woodbridge, New Jersey, at 9:00 a.m. As table 6.2 indicated, there were twenty-three speakers recognized and recorded at that hearing.

A very small number of speakers were recognized and recorded at all four public hearings as indicated in table 6.2 below.

The most striking point about those statistics was that of the 5.2 million registered voters in New Jersey and 5.7 million motorists residing in and tens of thousands passing through the state, only 110 speakers were scheduled and spoke during the four public hearings. That finding suggested that variables such as public notice, time and place, tightness of hearing schedule, complexity of the proposals and citizen apathy may have influenced participation in the hearings. Whatever the reason, as indicated in table 6.2 above, only 45 percent of the speakers favored the proposals and 35 percent opposed them. Not surprisingly, 21 percent of the speakers were undecided. Just as alarming was the fact that the fourth public hearing was held on the same day of and a few hours before the revised proposal's adoption. That action meant that the Authority was unlikely to incorporate those citizens' testimony into the final decision.

The proposals were overwhelming in that they contained $8 billion to almost $11 billion in construction projects and multilayered and multiyear toll increases. Those sophisticated and technical proposals may have confused and frustrated ordinary citizens. Thus, the governor, Commission,

Authority, and special interests dominated the hearing process. The voices of 110 citizens (the 61 percent who were either opposed to or undecided about the measure) appeared to be insufficient endorsement of such major proposals in a state of more than 8 million people. The Authority could have employed more inclusive methods like a referendum or deliberative forums. Perhaps, the crafters only desired to air the proposals in a controlled setting. In addition to the four public hearings, the Authority held a ten-day public comment period to allow the public to submit comments by e-mail, fax, and mail.

CORRESPONDENCE

The types of correspondence (electronic and otherwise) received and recorded by the NJTA included form statements, form letters, individual statements, and letters. There were 1,731 form statements signed and submitted to the NJTA in support of the initiative and 323 opposition form letters from the New Jersey Sierra Club. In addition, there were forty-two individuals submitting a statement of support, thirteen individuals submitting a letter of support, and eleven individuals submitting a form letter of support; there were seventy-one general support letters from major corporations and small business interests, sixty-nine from individuals, and nine from associations and interest groups; thirty letters or statements from individuals opposed the toll increases, and nine additional letters opposed the toll increases for environmental reasons.

It appeared that those who stood to benefit most, like employees and contractors, supported the proposals; and those whose benefits were remote or indirect or for whom the measure was against their will, ordinary citizens and environmentalists, opposed both proposals. That finding may not be startling, as individuals tended to support things that served their interests or those that suited their purposes, and vice versa. The majority of correspondence was form letters and form statements. That meant that organized interests on both sides of the initiative influenced or attempted to sway the proposals' final policy design more than any other entity, group, or citizen outside the crafters' domain. The collective voice of the ordinary citizen appeared to have been drowned out by those powerful political forces.

NJTA RESPONSE TO THE PUBLIC

In addition to the governor mandating a revision to the initial proposal as discussed above, the Authority prepared a written response to the public comments. The NJTA identified and responded to twelve issues arising from the public hearings and comment period. Issues extrapolated and framed by the NJTA included the Transportation Trust Fund, environmental concerns, economic concerns, Turnpike- and Parkway-widening projects, the Authority's finance issues, the Authority's ten-year capital plan, the ARC tunnel, comparison of the NJTA's rates with those of other jurisdictions, alternatives to the proposal, local traffic diversion, the trucking industry's concerns, and schedule/location of public hearings.

The Authority's written response to the public comments was terse and framed in such a way as to reflect favorably upon the agency. The statements revealed as little information as possible in addressing identified issues. Issues were identified and framed as though representative of all classes of commuters. The Authority's response was clinical, matter of fact, and carefully crafted not to stray away from message, to protect its position for the proposals. The response was presented in a fashion representative of a major corporation addressing customers or consumers on a picket line.

As another way to examine the influence of citizens on the policy decision, Dahl's (1998) principles on democratic process were applied to the New Jersey toll decision of 2008. Dahl's five principles for creating democratic process included effective participation of citizens, equality in voting, gaining enlightened understanding, final control over the agenda, and inclusion of adults.

EFFECTIVE PARTICIPATION

In 2008, New Jersey had a population of more than 8 million people, including 5.7 licensed drivers and 5.2 million registered voters. There were fewer than 115 citizens participating in four public hearings and fewer than 2,400 public comments submitted to the Authority. NJTA regulations (Subchapter 6 of NJTA Regulations 2004) stated that, "Any person may petition the Authority for the promulgation, amendment or repeal of any rule" (19:9.6.2) by NJTA. The regulations also stated that a hearing could be granted when fifty or more individuals or entities have expressed either the need for a public hearing on the rule or proposal or disagreement with the rule. Citizens participated at the formulation stage by voicing their opinions at the public hearings or submitting their comments to the Authority by e-mail, fax, or mail within a fixed ten-day period.

Citizens were reacting to a policy proposal already set by the Authority. The policy processes may have been efficient, as the NJTA held three public hearings in two days and another one sixteen days later, and held a ten-day comment period within thirty-two days; yet the processes were not effective or democratic in terms of citizen participation. According to Dahl (1998), effective participation means all citizens having equal and effective opportunities to make their views known before a policy was adopted. These statistics and findings suggested that the processes utilized by the Authority were not equal and effective, as required by Dahl.

Equality in Voting

In order to have equality in voting, Dahl (1998) required that all affected adults must have equal and effective vote on the final policy decision. The Authority did not present the policy proposal as a referendum, nor did citizens have an opportunity to vote on the measure otherwise. Citizens were permitted to respond to proposals drafted and presented by the Authority by voice or written statement only through four public hearings and during a ten-day public comment period. Not surprisingly, the political equality that Dahl (1998) addressed in his five principles for democratic process was not manifested fully in the New Jersey case. The mechanisms that the Authority employed for citizen participation were autocratic. Citizens were permitted to respond to policy proposals designed by the Authority and offered public participation opportunities in prescriptive ways. Neither the citizens of New Jersey nor the motorists using toll roads in the state designed or proposed any toll policy. The toll proposals were crafted and brought to them for comment.

Further, there was no obligation to do anything with the collected information other than retain it for public record. Citizens participated in the toll policymaking processes with political inequality and in less than effective ways. They were permitted to testify on the toll proposals but not to control the agenda nor make or vote on the final decision. Those important matters were left to the Commission. Citizens appeared to be beholden to those in power. In other words, citizens were depending upon the commissioners to consider and incorporate their concerns into the final policy decision. Consequently, the NJTA failed another Dahl (1998) tenet: "equality in voting."

GAINING ENLIGHTENED UNDERSTANDING

The toll proposals were contentious issues in that they attracted mass media attention at Commission meetings and the public hearings. They also spawned newspaper accounts, TV news reports, and radio talk-show commentary. Organized interests and the governor presented their stances on the initiative. Just 110 citizens spoke at the hearings and only 2,308 citizens corresponded during the comment period. However, most citizens participating in the processes were represented by organized interests (employees, contractors, businesses, or environmentalists). Proponents testified that the toll initiatives would benefit the state and citizens in terms of providing jobs, boosting the economy, and ensuring safety through improved and maintained infrastructure. Opponents offered counter testimony that the initiative was unnecessary, and would tax citizens, create more pollution and urban sprawl, and primarily benefit New York. However, all of those factors may have helped to create public awareness and understanding of the proposals. Therefore, by default, the public may have gained enlightened understanding and the Authority may have met that standard as required by Dahl (1998) in democratic processes.

FINAL CONTROL OVER THE AGENDA

There were five stages of policy development, ranging from agenda-setting to evaluation. The formulation stage was second in the process after agenda-setting. In general, business and industry, interest groups, and citizens were invited into the process at the formulation stage. Citizens were not involved in the toll policy decision at the agenda-setting stage. The other three stages were policy adoption, implementation, and policy evaluation (Anderson 2006, 4). It appeared that the governor, commissioners, and public administrators decided that tolls should be raised to meet its debt service obligations in 2009, to generate sufficient revenue for a ten-year capital plan, and to attract a $3 billion federal match for the ARC tunnel project. Because citizens were not engaged at the agenda-setting stage and were not in control of the agenda at any stage, the Authority failed to meet Dahl's (1998) tenet of having "citizens in final control over the agenda" in democratic processes. The processes for the 2008 toll initiative appeared to be controlled by the governor, commissioners, and the NJTA from beginning to end.

INCLUSION OF ADULTS

Evidence of citizen participation was found in the public hearing and public comment period processes that constituted the formulation stage. Citizens were given opportunities to react to toll proposals, voice their comments, or make statements through four public hearings and a public comment period. More specifically, citizens were given a chance to react to a policy decision already crafted by the governor, Commission, and Authority. In this instance, however, the Authority may have met Dahl's (1998) tenet dealing with inclusion of most adults. Most adults were given a window of thirty-two days in which to respond to the proposals. In other words, opportunities were provided for most adult citizens to voice their concerns, though one may question whether thirty-two days or the required forty-five-day notice constituted sufficient public notice or even met the effective participation standard.

INTERPRETATION OF FINDINGS

On September 23 and 24, 2008, the NJTA presented a toll increase proposal to the public. After the authority conducted three public hearings and received more than 2,300 public comments, Governor Corzine mandated a reduction in toll increases to lessen the burden on working families, and ordered a revised proposal be submitted to the public. The Authority carried out the governor's command and presented a revised proposal to the public on October 10, 2008. After hearing testimony from the public, the revised proposal was adopted the same day. In the initial proposal, the Authority's stated purposes were to certify that it would have sufficient revenue in 2009 to meet its debt service obligations, to fund a $9.7 billion capital plan, and to contribute $1.25 billion toward the tunnel project between New Jersey and New York. The revised proposal contained $7 billion in capital projects and $1.25 billion for the tunnel project.

A small number of citizens were involved in the toll policymaking processes through public hearings and a public comment period. Of the 5.7 million licensed drivers and the 5.2 million registered voters in the state, less than 115 spoke during the hearings and fewer than 2,400 submitted comments during the public comment period. For the most part, the governor, Commission, Authority, and organized interests, especially business and industry, and to lesser degree environmental organizations, dominated the policymaking processes. Ordinary citizens were marginalized as their voices were rarely heard.

There were only forty-nine testimonies in favor of the proposals at four public hearings and 1,946 public statements submitted in support. There were thirty-eight testimonies against the proposals during the public hearings and 362 public statements submitted in opposition to the proposals. There were twenty-three speaking during the public hearings who did not declare their position on the proposals. There were sixteen who spoke at two or more of the hearings.

The Authority revised its initial proposal after public input. It was not clear whether changes occurred as a result of public input or from some other political pressure or motivation. The initial proposal was revised by cutting $2.7 billion in capital projects. Interestingly, the ARC tunnel project remained intact at $1.25 billion. Probably, the Authority did not desire to risk losing the prospective $3 billion federal match. The Authority must have assumed it strategic to replace its number one purpose statement, "certifying sufficient revenue in 2009 to meet debt service obligations," with "placing the Authority on strong financial footing" (New Jersey Turnpike Authority 2008).

Nevertheless, upon reflection, the revised proposal revealed that the tunnel project may have been the driving force behind the toll initiative. The Authority implied that assertion in its Commission meeting on October 10, 2008, and in its written response to public comments that the $1.25 billion contribution must be in place in a timely manner or else it would lose the $3 billion federal matching funds. Perhaps the strategy for bringing forth a toll initiative at the time was raising the necessary capital commitment of $1.25 billion for the federal match.

The $9.7 billion and $7 billion capital plans may have provided the necessary smoke screen for tacit public approval of the tunnel project. If the tunnel project had been a stand-alone toll increase initiative, it would have been highly unlikely to generate sufficient public approval, and perhaps more likely would have evoked public outcry.

However, the Authority realized that there was no legal duty to gain public consent but only an obligation to serve notice or hold a public hearing forty-five days before implementation of the policy change. Even if there were overwhelming public outcry, the Authority still possessed the legal power to implement its policy decision after a public notice and hearing. In this case, though, the Authority did not have to face that challenge because of the small number of speakers attending the public hearings and the low number of citizens commenting during the public comment period, the majority of whom were generally in favor of the proposals.

SUMMARY

This case study was conducted through a qualitative content analysis of proposals, public comments, and records on the proposed toll increases and the Authority's response to them regarding the 2008 toll decision in New Jersey. Citizens were permitted to participate in the 2008 toll initiative at the formulation stage. There was little evidence that they participated at the agenda-setting stage or any other stage. The Authority held four public hearings and a public comment period within a thirty-two-day period. The NJTA requested citizens to attend the public hearings or submit their comments by e-mail, fax, or mail. The initiative was not put forward as a referendum, nor were citizens provided opportunities to vote on the measures otherwise. The NJTA regulations indicated voting privileges for the commissioners only.

Several scholars noted in this study have argued that the public hearing process was not an effective mechanism for citizen participation (Cole and

Caputo 1984; King et al. 1998). As seen in this case, the process was rendered inconsequential because the sponsoring agency was required only to conduct a hearing for the purpose of gaining public input and without the mandate of acting upon information heard or collected.

Public hearings as means for citizen participation were futile exercises when the sponsoring agency had no duty to act. In that scenario, citizens became objects that an agency could manipulate in its schemes. A hearing became a one-way communication process that suited the sponsor's aims, often at the expense of citizens. It was also one-sided, autocratic in nature, and tilted toward the agency's self-interest. The sponsor controlled the agenda, time and place, process, participants, and outcome. The rules of engagement were also under the sponsor's control.

The public hearings, though held at inconvenient times and places for working citizens, did provide limited opportunities for business and industry, special interests, and a small number of citizens to be heard. Correspondence (written communications in any form whether e-mailed, faxed, or mailed) was a weak form of citizen participation. It did not command urgency or guarantee that citizen voices were heard. Other than entering statements and documents into the public record, the correspondence, like the public hearings, served little useful purpose in affecting toll decisions. The governor, Commission, Authority, business and industry, and some special interest groups achieved their goals. Ordinary citizens appeared to have played minor roles in this particular case. Therefore, citizens were not effectively engaged in the toll policy decision as Dahl required, but they had some influence on the proposals. The governor did reduce the dollar amount of the final proposal however all of the major components of the original proposal remained intact.

The findings of this study suggested that the governor, Commission, and the Authority designed $11 billion and $8 billion toll proposals and presented them to the public. Affected citizens were allowed thirty-two days to consider and act upon the two major proposals presented to them. This window was not wide enough to constitute effective participation. A critical difference between the two proposals was the reduction in cost; however, the $1.25 billion for the ARC tunnel and the roadway widening and many repair projects remained intact. Whether the governor's decision to mandate that the toll proposal be cut and to offer discounts to seniors and others was swayed by citizen participation or was just a political ploy to attain his ends remained unknown. However, it was apparent that the beneficiaries supported the proposals and those without direct benefit opposed them.

The NJTA has not adopted effective mechanisms for involving citizens in its business affairs and operations. It has superficial methods and arrangements for citizen participation as described elsewhere in this study.

Chapter 7 explores the concept of justice and advances a theory of reparation. This chapter illuminates justice and proclaims justice as the end of state. It declares citizens as sovereign. It proposes a new construct of reparation as a remedy for righting wrongs perpetrated against certain classes of people, especially those of color.

Chapter 7

Justice and Democratic Citizenship

INTRODUCTION

The struggle for justice in America has been never ending for people of color and women. The fight for human and civil rights has been legendary. The crux of the problem has been in the elite class' quest to establish and maintain a homogenous society while those on the margins pursued a heterogeneous one. So, it has been the phenomenon of difference that caused tension in the United States. Many of America's social problems have emanated from this phenomenon. In this chapter, I argue that these challenges may be overcome through democratic citizenship. I define democratic citizenship in chapter 8 as the whole citizen participating in public life. I also posit here that a class of people wronged by society warrants compensation by the same through a theory of reparation.

Citizens have responsibilities to shape the form of state, to construct, reconstruct, destruct, support, or oppose a state. They also have a common duty to decide public laws, to hold public servants accountable, and to pursue the common good or its approximation. In essence, this is what the Founders may have had in mind when Thomas Jefferson was asked to write the Declaration of Independence in 1776. In the second paragraph of the Declaration, Jefferson stated:

> We hold these truths to be self-evident, that all men are created equal, that they are endowed by their Creator with certain unalienable Rights, that among these are Life, Liberty and the pursuit of Happiness. That to secure these rights, Governments are instituted among Men, deriving their just powers from the consent of the governed. That whenever any Form of Government becomes destructive of these ends, it is the Right of the People to alter or to abolish it,

> and to institute a new Government. (Second Continental Congress, Declaration, July 4, 1776)

Citizens as the proper authority of the state own all of its power and resources and therefore must consent on how the state is to be constituted, operated, and how they are to be governed. In a speech by Melancton Smith, an Anti-federalist, during the ratification of the U.S. Constitution, Smith declared:

> The fundamental principle of a free government, that the people should make the laws by which they were to be governed: He who is controlled by another is a slave; and that a government which is directed by the will of any one or a few, or any number less than is the will of the community, is a government for slaves. (Ketcham 2003, 341)

Citizens do not abdicate their basic rights no matter what form of democratic government or whether they exercise these rights or not. The primary purpose of a state is to pursue justice. In Federalist #51, James Madison stated, "Justice is the end of government. It is the end of civil society" (Ketcham 2003, 318). No just government acts against the "general will" of its people. So, if the primary duty of a state is to seek justice, then it must facilitate economic, social, political, and spiritual equality. Equality as understood here is equal opportunity and fairness in all four domains. All are equal in such a scheme.

A state has certain obligations to its citizens. The first order of state duties involves ensuring safety and protecting life; facilitating the provision of food, clothing, and shelter; and guaranteeing liberty. The citizens as the sole authority of a democratic state have obligations to the state and may delegate their duties to representatives or public servants. These duties include enlightening themselves, participating in public affairs, holding public servants accountable, and perpetuating the common good. A just state exists at the discretion of its citizens and the state's fiduciary obligation is to execute the general will or in its stead the approximate majority will of the people. It is incumbent upon democratic citizens to hold public officials accountable.

CONTROL OF GOVERNMENT

Control of government by holding public servants accountable is very important for American citizens. American citizens lay claim to this ideal as one of the core principles of democracy. Robert Dahl argued, "Democratic theory is concerned with processes by which ordinary citizens exert a relatively high degree of control over leaders" (Dahl 1998, 3). If this is so, perhaps these citizens are exercising their rights of guardianship and that these leaders are public servants to which they have some measure of control. Dahl posited, "Madison substantially accepted the idea that all the adult citizens of a republic must be assigned equal rights, including the right to determine the general direction of government policy" (Dahl 1998, 31). The problem lies, however, in the effective engagement of citizens in public policy decisions. Dahl stated, "A central guiding thread of American constitutional development has been the evolution of a political system in which all the active and legitimate groups in the population can make themselves heard at some critical stage in the process of decision" (Dahl 1998, 137). As Dahl made clear citizens need not only to be heard but for leaders to understand there are consequences. Dahl argued that "when I say that a group is heard effectively I mean more than the simple fact that it makes noise; I mean that one or more officials are not only ready to listen to the noise, but expect to suffer in some significant way if they do not placate the group, its leaders, or its most vociferous members" (Dahl 1998, 145).

Does a majority of citizens ever rule in a representative government? If not, then is majority rule a farce? Dahl postulated:

> If the majority rarely rules on matters of specific policy, nevertheless the specific policies selected by a process of "minorities rules" probably lie most of the time within the bounds of consensus set by the important values of the politically active members of the society, of whom the voters are a key group. If majorities in a democracy nearly always govern in the broad meaning of the term, they rarely rule in Madison's terms: for as we have seen, specific policies tend to be products of "minorities rule." The making of governmental decisions is not a majestic march of great majorities united upon certain matters of basic policy. It is the steady appeasement of relative small groups. Even when these groups add up to a numerical majority at election time it is usually not useful to construe that majority as more than an arithmetic expression. (Dahl 132-146)

In the sense in which Madison was concerned with the problem then, majority rule is mostly a myth. If placed in the context of Federalist philosophy, particularly, James Madison, it becomes a matter of majority rule versus minority rights. Dahl asserted, "Madisonian theory of democracy is an effort to bring off a compromise between the power of majorities and the power of minorities, between the political equality of all adult citizens on the one side, and the desire to limit their sovereignty on the other" (Dahl 4). If extended to its logical conclusion, would not any majority decision trample certain minority rights? Dahl posited, "Nearly all governmental actions deprive some individuals of legal rights they had previously possessed, and nearly all political groups seek some kind of governmental action that will deprive some individuals of certain existing legal rights" (Dahl 26).

Granted the republican form of governance is not perfect, however, it has stood the test of time. Dahl surmised:

> So long as the social prerequisites of democracy are substantially intact in this country, it appears to be a relatively efficient system for reinforcing agreement, encouraging moderation, and maintaining social peace in a restless and immoderate people operating a gigantic, powerful, diversified, and incredibly complex society. (Dahl 151)

MAKING CITIZENS WHOLE

In a democratic regime, the question is not whether a majority rule is better than minority rule or single rule, but whether a majority should rule in a just society. The majority of citizens in a democratic regime should govern even if their collective decisions are wrong, detrimental, or otherwise not beneficial to society-at-large. However, it would be unjust for the majority to abuse the minority or engage in wrongdoing. Minority rights must be respected in a just society. Arguably, in a republic, a majority has authority to err or make just and profitable decisions. In such a scheme the majority rules and the minority has rights. Madison was concerned about minority rights when he stated in Federalist #51, "If a majority be united by a common interest, the right of the minority will be insecure." The remedies for this phenomenon as stated by Madison were creating a "community will" independent of the majority or having many separate descriptions of citizens (Ketcham 2003, 318). I am not sure how separate descriptions of citizens would benefit the state except that a state could choose one among others in its schemes. In essence, include some and not others to suit its purposes.

In a tyrannical regime, an individual exercises power and control, and executes good and bad decisions. Therefore, the form of government is not the issue and it is not about what authority one or the other possesses but about justice. All three forms of government can bring about justice however majority rule is more likely to do so than the others. This appears to be true because a majority most likely has the propensity to represent general will or more closely approximate public interest. The majority is a check on "individual will."

The power and resources of the state reside in the people as well as the instrumentalities created and implemented upon their behalf. Citizens are the guardians of the state. Every citizen of a state is equal in the eyes of the law.

This means that his standing in a polity is no less or more than anyone else in the same political environment.

The second order of state duties is creating and maintaining conditions for citizens to experience full social, economic, political, and spiritual equality. Therefore, I have created a theoretical framework called the Citizen Equality Model for that purpose. I discuss this model in more detail in chapter 8. Consistent with John Rawls's *Theory of Justice*, discrimination against any citizen is permissible only if the least advantaged in a given society is the one most beneficial in such a scheme.

I have selected works of Plato, Aristotle, Thomas Hobbes, John Locke, Jean Jacques Rousseau, John Stuart Mill, Robert Dahl, and John Rawls to shed light on concepts of democracy, state, laws, and state of nature, social contract, liberty, and justice. A timeline is illustrated below in table 7.1 to provide an orientation on the evolution of Western political thought on these subjects beginning with Plato and Aristotle then skipping to Hobbes and ending with Rawls.

The notion of democratic governance has to do with the organization of state and civil society. Democratic governance is founded on the ideals of self-rule. Democracy is that form of government that places power in the hands of the people. In a direct democracy, the people rule and control their destinies in a civilized society. However, direct democracy works best with smaller populations in which the total citizenry decides on important public matters and opportunity exists for participation in public affairs is conveniently available. Robert Dahl (1998) argued that a democratic process includes five basic tenets: effective participation, equality in voting, gaining enlightened understanding, final control over the agenda, and inclusion of all or most adults. I elaborate on Dahl's theory in chapter 6.

With that said, operationalizing direct democracy becomes problematic in a state with a population over the tipping point where the population is

Table 7.1 Western Political Thought on Justice and Democracy

	Justice and Democracy	
Seminal Thinkers	*Era*	*Contribution*
1. Plato	427–347 BCE	The Republic of Plato
2. Aristotle	384–322 BCE	Politica and Ethica Nicomachea
3. Hobbes	1588–1679	Leviathan Parts I and II
4. Locke	1632–1704	Second Treatise of Government
5. Rousseau	1712–1788	On The Social Contract
6. Mill	1806–1873	Utilitarianism. On Liberty
7. Dahl	1915–2014	On Democracy. Preface to Democratic Theory
8. Rawls	1921–2002	Theory of Justice

Source: Constructed from the titles of their manuscripts indicated above and other sources.

too large in number for total citizen engagement in public affairs. Therefore, many variations of democracy have developed over time to approximate democracy or to characterize certain democratic governments. The more popular and successful one of these types is representative democracy or republican government, the one adopted by America and a number of other postmodern societies. A republican government is one that provides for representation through elected or appointed public officials. Therefore, representative democracy is the form of democratic governance implied in this chapter. Justice is discussed in the context of this type of regime.

On the question of justice, Plato argues doing good to friends and harming enemies based on their behaviors of good and evil (Cornford 1972, 13). This means rewarding a person's deeds with good for good and evil for evil. Further exploring the virtues of justice, Plato asserts that a person should be concerned with things he rightfully owns and possesses (Cornford 1972, 128). In other words, minding his own business is justice. Justice is the power that produces states and individuals (Cornford 1972, 141). This makes sense to the extent individuals are just since the same comprise states. Justice is innate—in the soul—and is a virtue of good. Unlike injustice which is more akin to a decease that harms the body (Cornford 1972, 143). Justice is doing what is right and never defrauding the blessings it produces (Cornford 1972, 347).

Aristotle, like Plato, posits that justice resides in the person. The disposition of character to do what is just and wish for the same (McKeon and Reeve 2001, 1002). According to Aristotle there are three manifestations of justice, including distribution of honor, money, and sharing something (McKeon and Reeve 2001, 1006). Equal is the operative word between two unequals where one is too much and the other is too little (McKeon and Reeve 2001, 1006). Justice does not exist outside of the law as the law determines what is just and unjust (McKeon and Reeve 2001, 112). Only through voluntary action does a person act justly or unjustly otherwise it is involuntary or incidental (McKeon and Reeve 2001, 1015).

Hobbes argues that a person is prohibited from harming himself and taking his life in a state of nature (Schneider 1958, 109). Further, life is paramount to all things but a person would be content to give as much freedom to others as he retains for himself to live in civil society (Schneider 1958, 110). No one should express hatred or contempt toward another; and everyone acknowledges that, by nature, all are equal. Hobbes asserts that no one has rights not enjoyed by the others and that persons should judge each other on the basis of equality (Schneider 1958, 120–128).

In *The Second Treatise of Government*, Locke argues that a person has perfect freedom in a state of nature and is bound by the law of nature—a state of equality—reciprocal, with no one having more than the other (Peardon1952,

4). Locke asserts that the compact does not end the state of nature but creates one body politic. Persons are still left free to make promises and agreements between themselves (Peardon 1952, 10). A person desires to be free and to be ruled only by the law of nature (Peardon 1952, 15). Locke posits that a person relinquishes natural liberty only by joining civil society (Peardon 1952, 54). According to Locke, the chief reason for persons uniting in commonwealths under government is the preservation of property (Peardon1952, 71). I am not sure that most under such circumstances would rank property over preservation of life.

Rousseau argues that a person agrees to leave the state of nature for mutual benefit under conditions equal for all (Bertram and Hoare 2012, 19). People come together as one body under the power and direction of the general will (Bertram and Hoare 2012, 20). Rousseau asserts that under this arrangement, people in the association are twice sovereign as private persons and members of the state (Bertram and Hoare 2012, 21). Among other things, there are two basic rewards of the social compact namely, civil liberty and property ownership (Bertram and Hoare 2012, 24).

In *Utilitarianism*, Mill argues no one should be deprived of his liberty or property or anything else which rightfully belong (Piest1957, 54). Mill asserts that it is just to give a person what he deserves and vice versa (Piest 1957, 55). There are three imperatives of justice namely, it is the right thing to do, wrong not to do, and it carries a moral claim (Piest 1957, 62). The notion of the social contract relies on a fictional agreement of an unknown period where all members in society agreed to obey the laws and consent to be punish otherwise (Piest 1957, 69). Mill posits that justice embodies moral rules for guiding life that reside in all persons (Piest 1957, 73).

In *A Theory of Justice*, Rawls argues that unjust institutions must be abolished, inviolability of certain rights, and equal citizenship (Rawls 1999, 3). According to Rawls, justice is a proper balance between competing claims relative to assigning rights and duties in the division of social advantages (Rawls 1999, 9). Further, the principles of justice are determined behind a "veil of ignorance" in the condition of the "original position" (Rawls 1999, 11–13). Simply put, all persons are equal with basic liberties, and social and economic inequalities are arranged to the greatest benefit of the least advantaged in society (Rawls 1999, 226).

This latter principle would prohibit any form of discrimination unless it benefits most the least advantaged members in society. So, disparities in the criminal justice system; admission and employment in all sectors; sales and rentals in the housing market; selling, trading, banking, and insuring in the financial markets; and providing education and healthcare would be prohibited unless the most disadvantaged persons in the society receive the greatest benefit. So, if injustice and inequality are bad and should not be tolerated, then those wronged should be appropriately compensated by necessity. I illustrate here the case of African descendants in America to further clarify this point.

THE PECULIAR CASE OF AFRICAN AMERICANS

African Americans were systematically oppressed and discriminated against in unique ways since their mass arrival in the United States in 1619. They were subjugated by the peculiar institutions of slavery, Jim Crow, and racial discrimination to the economic and social gain of others and the economic and social loss of their own. Kenneth Stamp argued:

> No specific date marked the legal establishment of chattel slavery in the South; but there were few obstacles in the way of its development. Neither the provisions of their charters nor the policy of the English government limited the power of colonial legislatures to control African American labor as they saw fit. [African Americans] did not have the benefit of written indentures that defined their rights and limited their terms of service. Their unprotected condition encouraged the trend toward special treatment, and their physical and cultural differences provided handy excuses to justify it. More than anything else, however, the landholders' growing appreciation of the advantages of slavery over older forms of servitude gave a power impetus to the growth of the new labor system. (Stamp 1956, 22)

W. E. B. Dubois asserted, "We must remember the black worker was the ultimate exploited; that he formed that mass of labor which had neither wish nor power to escape from labor status" (Dubois 1962, 15).

During the post-bellum South immediately following the Reconstruction era, time did not improve matters.

> Between 1890 and 1910, African Americans were systematically disenfranchised by various political schemes ranging from the revision of state constitutions to requiring poll taxes, literacy tests, and property qualifications, to creation of all-white Democratic primaries. . . . Accompanying disenfranchisement were increased Jim Crow segregation laws in both public and private institutions and facilities and also the virtual collapse of public education and the systematic exclusion by white laborers of African Americans from jobs in the skilled occupational ranks they had held since slavery (such as barbering, masonry, brick laying, carpentry, and the better agricultural jobs). (Wilson 1980, 58–59)

It would be difficult for a rational person, who is knowledgeable of American history, to refute the above historical situations. However, a growing number of persons would espouse the view that things have really changed since the Civil Rights movement of the 1950s and 1960s and argue that race is no longer a significant factor in determining life chances of African Americans especially in the age of Barack Obama. "Racial discrimination—through legalized segregation in the 19th and first half of the 20thcentury and through de facto segregation and discrimination that persist today—is a clear driver of economic inequality in the US" (Stiglitz 2016, 49).

Theoretically, as a class, African Americans will remain at a disadvantage as long as they do not have control of significant wealth and power. In order for African Americans to gain power and wealth, the business community must change to the extent that corporations and markets are free and open. In corporate boardrooms, "ladders" and "doors" at all levels must be accessible and open to all and "glass ceilings" must disappear. To a significant degree, African Americans are still the "last hired and the first fired." Effectively, the majority of African Americans are still shut out of the economic mainstream. In a capitalistic society such as the one we have in the United States, a person is not free to enjoy life, liberty, and the pursuit of happiness without the financial means to do so. Elites have capitalized on the legacy of slavery and racial oppression and created, dominated, and monopolized the means of production and the markets of wealth to the detriment of others, including poor whites who make up the majority of poor people in America.

Let us not forget that while African Americans were enslaved and forced to help cultivate and manufacture the wealth that some elites control and enjoy today, it was done at their own expense and demise. "First, African workers had been transmuted by the perverted canons of mercantile capitalism into property. Then, African labor power as slave labor was integrated into organic composition of nineteenth century manufacturing and industrial capitalism" (Robinson 1983, 113). The cumulative effects of slavery, racial oppression, and Jim Crowism have placed others at an economic and social advantage and relegated African Americans, as a class, to an economic and social disadvantage.

A THEORY OF REPARATION

The inheritance of an economic gain or loss is very determinative. In the case of African Americans, as a class, they are marginalized and trapped in a perpetual position of playing catch-up, as the unjust economic system continues to evolve farther away from their grasp; while simultaneously, great economic and social advantages continue to appreciate in value and return great dividends to other heirs.

For example, the typical family passes wealth and its dividends and residuals from one generation to the next. Each succeeding generation has the advantage of family inheritance as a foundation on which to erect its livelihood. If one generation fails to maintain or appreciate its inheritance then the succeeding generation has to rebuild, and its posterity suffers a significant loss.

However, if a successive generation builds upon its inheritance by generating additional wealth it may either enjoy as good or better than quality of life and standard of living vis-à-vis its ancestors. The underlying assumption here is that no artificial roadblocks are encountered by a particular generation. If artificial roadblocks or other handicaps are encountered by a particular generation then each succeeding generation incurs a loss. The cumulative effect of this phenomenon on succeeding generations may be calculated in financial terms similar to the theory of time value of money. Shim and Siegel argue, "A dollar now is worth more than a dollar later. . . . Money has a time value. . . . A dollar in hand today is worth more now than a dollar to be received tomorrow because of the interest it could earn if it were put into a savings account or investment account. Compounding interest means interest earns interest" (Shim and Siegel 1997, 284).

Yet a more appropriate way to view reparation is the present value theory. In short, this theory may be illustrated as "the present value of X dollars to be received in n years from now at a simple interest rate r is obtained by solving the equation $X = PV(1 + r)n$" (Hyman 2005, 227). It may be applied to any type of cause for reparation (slavery, reservation, holocaust, internment camp, segregation, incarceration, or maltreatment) and the approximate present value can be known. "At the beginning of the nineteenth century, one bought an average slave for \$200; while in 1860 the price ranged from \$1,400 to \$2,000" (Dubois 1962, 13). If a dollar value is placed on property, labor, or wrong at a given time and calculated over a period of time at a certain rate with interest earned then one may ascertain the approximate loss or gain for a particular generation or class of people or individual.

Each incidence of economic discrimination or wrong causes an adverse chain reaction on a particular future generation. The economic loss created by this kind of incident is not recoverable. It is a permanent loss whereas the talents, thriftiness, frugality, or any other positive variables do not matter. The economic gain is forgone and does not contribute to future gains. As to specific economic losses incurred, such as the quality and quantity of personal and real property, that is, home, car, land, and so on, a particular generation or class may purchase or own are decisive. Another economic loss may be the quality and quantity of education a generation or class may afford. Still other examples may include the quality and quantity of vacation that one may be able to enjoy.

Another example of economic loss may be the quality of healthcare a class may be able to purchase. Other examples include the quality and volume of food and clothing a class can afford. If viewed in this context, one readily discerns the devastating and costly impact of economic loss on a particular class or generation. Each generation inherits a social and economic gain or loss. The ramification of such gains and losses determines the life chances of each succeeding generation. In a capitalistic economy such as the United States, one's economic worth defines quality of life and standard of living boundaries.

SUMMARY

Citizens are the guardians of the democratic state. This means that citizens have the ultimate authority to decide what form of government they choose to construct and how they are to be governed. The end of state is justice. Justice is fairness; and doing what is right. This means among other things giving each what he deserves. If one or more person experience(s) wrongdoing, then reparation is the appropriate remedy as described above.

In short, I do not believe that a group of individuals originally designed the system to have such an effect but once the situation manifested itself, those in power cultivated and exploited it. The just remedy to this problem would be a redistribution of wealth, the creation of a level playing field, which means starting all over at square one. Short of this remedy, African Americans and others born or naturalized in the United States, similarly situated as classes, will never reach or equal that of elites in terms of social and economic status. As a footnote, I do not expect elites to voluntarily agree with this remedy. If African Americans and others similarly situated are to achieve parity in this capitalistic society, they must find effective ways of doing so. Integrating a person's space or even changing a person's views toward you will not necessarily motivate him to equitably share his privilege, power, and wealth with you, or even consider you an equal. The state must make citizens whole by creating and maintaining conditions for full social, economic, political, and spiritual equality.

Chapter 8 explores the problematic concept of citizenship in America. The chapter draws attention to salient issues associated with citizenship, advances legal citizenship status, discusses several models of citizenship, and offers a framework for a new theory of citizenship.

Chapter 8

Democratic Citizenship and America

INTRODUCTION

Citizenship is still a coveted status in America. It is one of the most important standings in our civil society. By this I mean full legal citizenship with all of its rights, privileges, duties, and responsibilities—a whole citizen. In general, those persons with this status have opportunity for access to "the good life" and those without are often demonized, marginalized, or otherwise discriminated against and barred from the same. "The good life" as meant here is the enjoyment of life, liberty, and the pursuit of happiness.

In this chapter, I provide a brief overview of citizenship and identify salient challenges that weaken democratic citizenship in America. Here democratic citizenship is understood as the whole citizen engaged in public life. Specifically, this discourse captures the contested nature of nation-state citizenship and the prevailing issues associated with it that threaten democracy in America. I also make the case for legal citizenship status. In addition, I discuss a few citizenship models and advance a framework for a theory of democratic citizenship. I call this theory the "Citizen Equality Model" (CEM). This model involves four properties of equality: political, social, economic, and spiritual. I argue that a citizen is not whole when missing or deficient in any one of these properties.

The challenges to citizenship in America are complex. First, beyond legal status (born or naturalized), there are other ambiguous expressions of the meaning of citizen. Second, in a nation where demographics continue to shift, immigration has become ever more a salient political issue. Conjoined with the confluence of challenges brought by globalization and digitization, the immigration issue weakens nation-state citizenship status. Third, noncitizens pose an imminent danger as they are outcast into the shadows of civil society. This condition is artificial as it is created under suspicious circumstances. Why do we choose certain people over others? Why build bridges to some countries and construct walls between others?

In Athens, Greece (between 500 and 300 BCE), there is a documented ancient history on citizenship; "citizen" applied solely to white males of the ruling class. Only those in this elite group of citizens could fully participate in what the Greeks called "democracy," and decide on public matters applicable to all. In 2007, Raaflaub, Ober, and Wallace argued "this minority body was composed of adult male citizens" (Raaflaub et al. 2007, 11). Very few persons were considered citizens in most regimes. Janoski asserted that "citizenship rights applied to less than a tenth of the population in many nations" (Janoski 1998, 3). The leading class of every era reconstructed a narrative on citizenship. In 2002, Isin posited that "the history of citizenship has been narrated by dominant groups who articulated their identity as citizens and constituted strangers, outsiders, and aliens as those who lacked the properties for citizenship" (Isin 2002, ix). Isin stated further that "throughout centuries alienating strategies and technologies of citizenship, such as stigmatization, marginalization, heroization, ritualization, professionalization, universalization, confratization, and mediatization, constituted citizens as those who managed to inculcate virtues through others as outsiders" (Isin 2002, ix). Others such as "slaves, women, peasants, artisans, prostitutes, vagabonds and workers were considered problematized beings" (Isin 2002, ix). Citizenship was tied to race, masculinity, wealth, and city-state.

In 1868, Congress passed the Fourteenth Amendment stating, among other things, that all persons born or naturalized in the United States are citizens. Operationally though, persons of Native American, African, Asian, or Hispanic descents, and women were excluded from full citizenship. These disenfranchised groups gradually gained more equitable measures of civil rights and immunities after long periods of time. Throughout U.S. history, "lawmakers structured US citizenship in terms of illiberal and undemocratic racial, ethnic and gender hierarchies" (Smith 1985, 1). Nearly 250 years after Thomas Jefferson penned the Declaration of Independence, and more than 225 years since the Framers signed and the states ratified the U.S. Constitution, and more than 155 years after slavery, the debate on citizenship remains unsettled in America.

Although Congress enacted the Fifteenth Amendment in 1870 granting citizens the right to vote without regard to race, color, or previous condition of servitude, the old concept of citizenship did not effectively change in the Western world (except during the Reconstruction era) until later nineteenth and early twentieth centuries (CE) when European nations and America more broadly opened voting to persons of color and women. Historically, American law was rife "with forms of second-class citizenship, denying most of the adult population of personal liberties or opportunities for political participation on the basis of race, ethnicity, gender, and religion" (Smith 1985, 2). Caucasian women were legally and politically enfranchised in the United States a century ago (1920 through the Nineteenth Amendment) and descendants of slaves approximately fifty-five years ago (1965 through the Voting Rights Act) (Raaflaub et al. 2007, 12). By the early twenty-first century, the vast majority of the population of European states and North America was theoretically entitled to vote (Fahrmeir 2007, 7). The norm was that "large portions of the population were not seen or heard in the halls of power in America. Those persons were not able to shape their collective fates" (Smith 1985, 7).

During the later quarter of the twentieth and beginning of the first quarter of the twenty-first centuries the concept of citizenship changed again. Largely influenced by immigration, globalization, and digitization, citizenship would no longer be wholly associated with nation-states. Persons would no longer be bound by location alone but through ties to global communities as well; therefore, more broadly operationalizing the concept of global citizenship. However, this concept was more theoretical than practical.

America has struggled with whom to grant full citizenship since its founding in 1776. Native Americans (who inhabited North America for centuries prior to European invasion) were largely relegated to reservations under the Indian Removal Act of 1830. Persons of African descent were enslaved up to 1863 (freed in rebellious states through the Emancipation Proclamation) but denied full citizenship until 1965, and still continue to confront discrimination in many important respects even today.

In effect, Caucasian women were given the right to vote in 1920 through the Nineteenth Amendment but denied equal pay until recently. Asian descendants were permitted only to work hard labor upon arrival in the early 1800s; and under the Chinese Exclusion Act of 1882, a ten-year moratorium was placed on Chinese labor; they still continue to face discriminatory practices regarding citizenship and in other spheres in American life. In 1907, immigration restrictions were in place on Japanese people and some were ordered to attend Asiatic schools in California. By Executive Order (Japanese Relocation Order), Japanese Americans and those of Japanese descent (roughly 112,000 people) were placed in internment camps in 1942 during World War II. Under the Immigration Act of 1924, the law and practice systematically favored certain European countries to the detriment of others.

Smith posited "many of the restrictions on immigration, naturalization, and equal citizenship seemed to express views of American civic identity that did not feature either individual rights or membership in a republic" (Smith 1985, 2). Hispanics and Latinos were barred under discriminatory policies and practices as late as the passing of the 1965 Immigration Act and the lingering effects of this legacy still remain as imminent threats today. Further, Vietnamese, Haitian, and Cuban immigrants and refugees were similarly situated. Recently, millions of persons of Hispanic descent have been denied citizenship, and resident aliens (largely Hispanic) were marginalized, ostracized, and deported each year.

CITIZEN AMBIGUITY

The ambiguous nature of the meaning of "citizen" creates problems in deciding who are and who are not citizens in a nation-state. Fahrmeir argued, "The meaning of citizenship is not only contested, it has also become quite diffuse" (Fahrmeir 2007, 1). More recently, primarily accelerated by globalization and digitization, the term *citizen* took on new meanings. In addition to legal status, "citizen" is now associated with political and community identities. How these other meanings of citizenship operationalize when contested varies upon circumstances and the environments where they happen.

Legal status is granted by an authority; political and community identities may be assumed through customs, norms, and associations. Fahrmeir asserted that "formal citizenship is: the legal definition of a close relationship between individuals and one state, usually documented in passports or other citizenship certificates" (Fahrmeir 2007, 2). Smith posited, "Citizenship is more than legal status and at a minimum a statement of political and personal identity that evokes complex, powerful and often conflicting ideas and sentiments" (Smith 1985, 1). Isin and Turner argued, "Citizenship is both legal status that confers an identity on persons and a social status that determines how economic and cultural capital are redistributed and recognized within society" (Isin and Turner 2007, 14).

In 1984, Barber stated that "to be a citizen is to be a party to the social contract and thus to be a legal person" (Barber 1984, 218). In addition, Barber asserted that "citizens are autonomous persons whom participation endows with a capacity for common vision" (Barber 1984, 232). Another view posited by Janoski was "citizenship is passive and active membership of individuals in a nation-state with certain universalistic rights and obligations at a specified level of equality" (Janoski 1998, 9). In sum, Barbieri argued that citizenship "refers to a status employed to classify people, a form of membership, a legal and political identity often referencing a nationality;

and it indicates an ideal or virtue or type of responsibility involving public-spiritedness or patriotism" (Barbieri 1998, 3).

LEGAL CASTE SYSTEM

There is no longer a legal caste system in the United States where citizenship was hierarchical from noncitizenship to partial citizenship to full citizenship and codified by law. In America, prior to 1965, everything was segregated from family to community and from state to federal government. Although slavery in America can be traced back to 1619, from 1776 until 1863 the United States maintained a system of slavery and a caste system. The racial caste system in the United States has evolved from one of slavery to Jim Crow to mass incarceration (Alexander 2012, 219).

At the bottom of the pyramid were slaves, in the middle were indentured servants, which included poor whites, and at the top were white Anglo-Saxon Protestants. Corresponding rights and privileges were associated with each group. The Supreme Court ruled in 1857 in *Dred Scott*, among other things, "that Negroes could not become citizens of the United States and thus could not sue in Federal court" (Finkelman 1985, 47). And in 1896, in the case of *Plessy v. Ferguson* (regarding Homer Plessy, a Negro) the court held that public accommodations could be "separate but equal."

In spite of the Civil Rights Act of 1866 and the passage of Amendments 13, 14, and 15, and after the Reconstruction period (ended 1877), the United States instituted a system of racial segregation (de facto slavery) that did not begin to dismantle until 1954 with the *Brown* decision and culminated with passage of the Civil Rights Act of 1964 and the Voting Rights Act of 1965. Not surprising, vestiges of this old system remain in effect. Further, since the 1960s the American economic system has created a well-defined class system. So, in effect, there is a de facto caste system of class, race, and gender structured by economics that still remains today.

However, America has become more civilized over time permitting a majority of persons living in the country opportunities to enjoy full citizenship status. The U.S. population is now 309 million (according to the 2010 census), including 85 million (27 percent) people of color. In 1960, the U.S. population was 179 million (1960 census) with 20 million (11 percent) people of color. This growth and shift in population toward people of color has alarmed many European Americans accustomed to the old norm. Too, it is important to note that the notion of citizenship has evolved over time. Citizen is more than legal status. It is not etched in stone. We live in a global society only through Internet and social media. The postmodern age is in full bloom. People can hold instant communication with one another worldwide.

NONCITIZENS

There are essentially two ways to attain citizenship in America: natural birth or naturalization. If one were born in the country or its declared territories or abroad to one or both citizen parent(s), one would automatically be a citizen of the United States. In order to become naturalized, one must meet a residency requirement, pass a citizenship exam, pledge allegiance to the United States at a swearing in ceremony, and pay naturalization fees ($725.00) (A Guide to Naturalization U.S. Citizenship and Immigration Services, M-476 [rev.11/16]). For all intents and purposes, there are several types of persons living in the United States: persons born or naturalized in the country, and those who are neither of the above. The first two groups are considered citizens; members of the latter group are referred to as "noncitizens."

Noncitizens are identified as "illegal aliens," or undocumented persons, in the eyes of the law. *Alien* refers to a person who is not a national of the state where he or she is present (*United Nations Declarations on Human Rights of Individuals, 1985*). (See table 8.1.) Table 8.1 describes the rights of nonnationals as declared by the United Nations. These persons are subject to detainment, deportation, or incarceration if discovered by law enforcement officials for any violation of the law of which they have been charged and held accountable.

In 1998, Barbieri asserted that "these minorities consist primarily of migrant laborers—guest workers—and their families and more recently include illegal immigrants and refugees fleeing perils" (Barbieri 1998, 1). Some of these noncitizens (migrant workers and guest workers) have been granted status to work in the United States. In 2013, "almost 3,100 foreigners per day received immigrant visas or green cards that allowed them to live, work, and become naturalized citizens after 5 years" (Martin 2013, 6).

Work permits and green cards are granted for that purpose. However, generally speaking, the status of noncitizens was not the same as those visiting or working or being educated in the United States with visas (official visitors). This means that noncitizens may not have the educational, employment, housing, medical, or voting privileges as do most U.S. citizens. There are exceptions to the rule, but the vast majority of noncitizens are trapped in the "twilight zone" of civil society.

Those without citizenship status are exposed to all sorts of risks and dangers. The most prominent risks being detainment and deportation. Some other dangers include incarceration, domestic slavery, and sex and drug trafficking. Further, noncitizens are shackled by the lack of basic rights and privileges,

Table 8.1 Declaration on the Human Rights of Individuals Who Are Not Nationals of the Country in Which They Live (1985)

1. Alien shall apply to any individual who is not a national of the state in which he or she presides.
2. This Declaration shall not be interpreted as legitimizing illegal entry nor shall any provision be interpreted as restricting the right of any state to promulgate laws and regulations concerning the entry of aliens.
3. Such laws and regulations shall not be incompatible with international legal obligations of the state.
4. This Declaration shall not prejudice the rights accorded by domestic or international laws the state is obliged to accord to aliens.
5. Every state shall make public its national legislation or regulations affecting aliens.
6. Aliens shall observe the laws of a state and regard with respect the customs and traditions of the people of that state.
7. Aliens shall enjoy the right to life and security of person; and no alien shall be subject to arbitrary arrest and detention; no alien shall be deprived of his or her liberty except as established by law.
8. Aliens shall enjoy the right to protection against arbitrary or unlawful interference with privacy, family, home, or correspondence.
9. Aliens shall enjoy the right to be equal before the courts, tribunals, and all other authorities administering justice; to free assistance of an interpreter in criminal proceedings and when prescribed by law other proceedings.
10. Aliens shall enjoy the right to choose a spouse, to marry, to found a family.
11. Aliens shall enjoy the right to freedom of thought, opinion, conscience, and religion subject only to limitations prescribed by law.
12. Aliens shall enjoy the right to retain their own language, culture, and tradition.
13. Aliens shall enjoy the right to transfer abroad earnings, savings or other monetary assets, subject to domestic currency regulations.
14. Aliens shall enjoy the right to leave the country.
15. Aliens shall enjoy the right to freedom of expression.
16. Aliens shall enjoy the right to peacefully assembly.
17. Aliens shall enjoy the right to own property.
18. Aliens shall enjoy the right to liberty of movement and freedom to choose their residence.
19. Subject to national legislation, the spouse and minor children of a lawful alien shall be admitted to accompany, join, and stay with the alien.
20. No alien shall be subjected to torture or cruel, inhuman or degrading treatment or punishment; no alien shall be subjected without his or her free consent to medical or scientific experimentation.
21. A lawful alien may be expelled from a state in accordance to the law; and shall be allowed to submit reasons on the contrary and be represented for that purpose. Individual or collective expulsion of such aliens on the grounds of race, color, religion, culture, descent or national or ethnic origin is prohibited.
22. Aliens shall enjoy the right to safe and healthy working conditions, to fair wages and equal remuneration for work of equal value.
23. Aliens shall enjoy the right to join trade unions and other organizations or associations of their choice and participate in their activities.
24. Aliens shall enjoy the right to health protection, medical care, social security, social services, education, rest and leisure as provided under relevant regulations.
25. No alien shall be arbitrarily deprived of his or her lawfully acquired assets.
26. Any alien shall be free to communicate with consulate or diplomatic mission or representative of the state of which he or she is a national.

Source: Excerpted and summarized from Declaration of Human Rights of Individuals Who Are Not Nationals of the Country in Which They Live (1985).

such as voting and eligibility for government assistance (e.g., student aid, food stamps, and healthcare). The bottom line: if persons do not have full legal citizenship in America, their status becomes circumspect and inconsequential in public life, with very little control over the politics that affects their daily life. In effect, they become persons relegated to the margins of society; often times finding themselves residing in the shadows of civil society.

LEGAL STATUS

Full legal citizenship gives one unobstructed access to life, liberty, and pursuit of happiness, not be impeded by artificial barriers or impairments. These rights and immunities allow one to enjoy freedom of speech, association, assembly, religion, protest, and pursuit of dreams (see table 8.2). Table 8.2 describes the rights and immunities of citizenship afforded citizens by the U.S. Constitution.

Table 8.2 Full Citizenship Permits the Following Rights and Immunities

1. Age 25 years and 7 years, a citizen eligible to be a Representative (Art. 1 Sec. 1)
2. Natural-born citizen eligible to be President, at least age 35, with 14 years residence (Art. 2 Sec. 1)
3. Entitled to all privileges and immunities of citizens (Art. 4 Sec. 2)
4. Right to petition the government (1st Amend.)
5. Right to peaceably assemble (1st Amend.)
6. Right to free speech (1st Amend.)
7. Right to practice religion (1st Amend.)
8. Right of the people to keep and bear arms (2nd Amend.)
9. Right against soldiers occupying your home except as provided by law (3rd Amend.)
10. Right against unreasonable search and seizure (4th Amend.)
11. Right not to answer for a capital or infamous crime (5th Amend.)
12. Right not to be held in double jeopardy (5th Amend.)
13. Right not to be compelled to witness against self (5th Amend.)
14. Right to a speedy and public trial by an impartial jury (6th Amend.)
15. Right to trial by jury (7th Amend.)
16. Right against excessive bail, excessive fines, and cruel and unusual punishment (8th Amend.)
17. Right against slavery or involuntary servitude, unless punishment for a convicted crime (13th Amend.)
18. Right against depriving any person of life, liberty, or property, without due process of law (14th Amend.)
19. All persons born or naturalized in the U.S. are citizens. (14th Amend.)
20. Right against abridging the privileges or immunities of citizenship (14th Amend.)
21. Right to equal protection of the laws (14th Amend.)
22. Right to vote (15th, 19th, 24th, 26th Amend.)

Source: Excerpted and paraphrased from the U.S. Constitution as amended.

In a legal sense, citizenship means the rights, privileges, duties, and responsibilities bestowed upon a person by an authority governing the jurisdiction where a person resides. In the United States, this authority belongs to the federal government. Once citizenship has been bestowed upon a person, the same becomes a recognized citizen. The challenges to legal status threaten nation-state citizenship because they negate the state's claim to a populous of patriots. Smith argued, "Aspirants to power require a population to lead that imagines itself to be a people; and they need a people that imagines itself in ways that make leadership by those aspirants appropriate" (Smith 1985, 6).

In short, if a nation has no loyal and literate citizens, it has no enlightened patriots to defend itself against threats. In such a situation, the nation-state is at risk. Patriots must protect and serve the common good. Patriots who do not think through and weigh policy alternatives or judge the character and fitness of a political candidate or party to ascertain which better serves their interests are gullible to the whims of either to their detriment. Patriots must be informed to be democratic citizens. Democratic institutions are made vulnerable through populations that do not understand and claim their political place and space in public life. If democratic governance is to best serve the people, the people must be able to recognize their interests and act upon their interests. This constitutes the essence of democratic citizenship. Democracy requires active citizenship. Active citizenship is not a politics of grand overcoming, but rather ongoing struggle against limitation and imperfection (Barker 2009, 5).

In a nation governed by laws, what does it mean to be a person without legal status? Without the legal status of citizenship, a person residing or operating in a jurisdiction of the United States is merely a human being who may be entitled to rights and privileges adopted by the United Nations in the *Universal Declaration of Human Rights* (1948). (See table 8.3.) Table 8.3 describes rights and privileges afforded all persons as human beings as declared by the United Nations.

In addition, noncitizens may be protected by the *Declaration of Human Rights for Individuals* as noted previously. Only sovereign authorities, such as a state or ruling body, can grant citizenship status. Barbieri posited that "because they do not possess citizenship, they are blocked from political membership. . . . They are cosigned instead to a sort of political limbo, a perpetual state of partial membership and disenfranchisement" (Barbieri 1998, 2). To call oneself a citizen without the rights and immunities of citizenship is meaningless in a state except where human rights are recognized. It is tantamount to being a trespasser.

In a typical trespassing case, the landowner has the right to remove the trespasser from his property. However, one may argue that a state is a public

Table 8.3 The Universal Declaration of Human Rights

1. All human beings are born free and equal in dignity and rights.
2. Everyone is entitled to all the rights and freedoms set forth in this declaration.
3. Everyone has the right to life, liberty, and security of person.
4. No one shall be held in slavery or servitude.
5. No one shall be subjected to torture or to cruel, inhuman, or degrading treatment or punishment.
6. Everyone has the right to recognition everywhere as a person before the law.
7. All are equal before the law and are entitled without any discrimination to equal protection of the law.
8. Everyone has a right to an effective remedy by the competent national tribunals for acts violating the fundamental rights granted him by the constitution or by law.
9. No one shall be subjected to arbitrary arrest, detention, or exile.
10. Everyone is entitled in full equality to a fair and public hearing by an independent and impartial tribunal.
11. Everyone charge with a penal offense has a right to be presumed innocent until proved guilty according to law in a public trial. No one shall be held guilty of any penal offense on account of any act or omission which did not constitute a penal offense.
12. No one shall be subjected to arbitrary interference with his privacy nor to attacks upon his honor and reputation.
13. Everyone has the right to freedom of movement and residence. Everyone has the right to leave any country and to return to his country.
14. Everyone has the right to seek and to enjoy in other countries asylum from persecution.
15. Everyone has the right to a nationality. No one shall be arbitrarily deprived of his nationality nor denied the right to change his nationality.
16. Men and women of full age have a right to marry and to found a family.
17. Everyone has the right to own property. No one shall be arbitrarily deprived of his property.
18. Everyone has the right to freedom of thought, conscience, and religion.
19. Everyone has the right to the freedom of opinion and expression.
20. Everyone has the right to freedom of peaceful assembly and association. No one may be compelled to belong to an association.
21. Everyone has the right to take part in the government of his country. Everyone has the right of equal access to public service in his country.
22. Everyone has the right to social security.
23. Everyone has the right to work.
24. Everyone has the right to equal pay for equal work. Everyone who works has the right to just and favorable remuneration. Everyone has the right to form and to join trade unions.
25. Everyone has the right to rest and leisure.
26. Everyone has the right to a standard of living adequate for the health and well-being of himself and of his family.
27. Motherhood and childhood are entitled to special care and assistance.
28. Everyone has the right to education. Parents have a prior right to choose the kind of education that shall be given to their children.
29. Everyone has the right freely to participate in the cultural life of the community, to enjoy the arts, and to share in scientific advancement and its benefits. Everyone has the right to the protection of the moral and material interests resulting from any scientific, literary, or artistic production of which he is the author.
30. Everyone is entitled to a social and international order in which the rights and freedoms set forth in this Declaration can be fully realized.
31. Everyone has duties to the community in which alone the free and full development of his personality is possible.

Source: The Universal Declaration of Human Rights as adopted by members of the United Nations in 1948 (summarized by the author).

domain. The counterargument is yes, but the state controls the public domain and may require persons to adhere to regulations that restrict and prohibit certain individuals, acts, and behaviors. Some restrictions may include banning minors, weapons, pets, loitering, loud music, and noise in public facilities, and prohibiting visitors after business hours. Or, in this case the trespasser may be arrested, detained, and deported. A person without legal citizenship status eventually finds himself encumbered in public life. Legal status or formal nation-state relationship is the strongest claim for citizenship.

IMMIGRATION

Citizenship has become very problematic because there are significant populations residing and operating in the United States without the legal status of citizenship. There are roughly 12 million undocumented or illegal aliens in America. The number of unauthorized foreigners peaked at 12.2 million in 2007 and fell by 1 million during the recession of 2008 (Martin 2013, 6). The politicization of immigration has been a historic problem for citizenship status in the United States. Perhaps an important question to raise is because "political membership is a human creation, a status we grant to ourselves, why it is given to some and not others?" (Barbieri 1998, 1).

Historically, the policies and practices regarding citizenship admissions appeared racist and unjust. "The process of achieving personhood frequently requires acts of allegiance to the nation-state, which entails the rejection or downplaying of past cultural or national memberships" (Janoski 1998, 8). Evidence shows that country of origin weighed favorably or unfavorably on application for citizenship until passage of the Immigration Act of 1965. Immigration law changed in 1965 . . . natural origin preference that favored entry of Europeans was dropped (Martin 2013, 5). The million-dollar question is, has the discriminatory practice changed? For example, historically, persons from European countries were privileged over those from Africa and China. Thousands of European descendants were admitted annually into the country and undocumented Europeans were not considered a major issue.

Today, people are connected worldwide through advancements in technology that enable them to use communication devices for that purpose. The advent of digitization, through communication devices like cell phones, personal computers, television, and related platforms, enable citizens across the world to communicate in real time. Now families, friends, and strangers can interact with one another for social, business, political, and spiritual purposes at any time. Therefore, boundaries created by nation-states now have limited meaning and effect. Through Internet and social media people are free to have global relationships and experiences regardless of location or citizenship status.

CITIZENSHIP MODELS

To provide a structural understanding of how citizenship has been viewed in postmodernity, I describe, compare, and contrast Benjamin Barber's (1984) forms of citizenship model, Terry Cooper's (1984) model of legal and ethical citizenship, and Thomas Bryer and Sofia Prysmakova-Rivera's (2018) three forms of citizenship model. All of these models in some nuanced ways relate to parts of my CEM, which will be discussed later. The CEM is different than these three models in that its primary focus is on the constitutive qualities (economic, political, social, and spiritual) that every person must possess to acquire full equality in a capitalistic-republican government.

Barber's model recognizes three kinds of democracy (representative, unitary, and strong) that prescribes a secondary role for citizens. One is the representative, or thin, democracy that envisions a social contract that authorizes a sovereign to govern citizens on their behalf. Another is a unitary democracy arrangement rooted in the notion of citizens as blood brothers united by genetics. The other is strong democracy in which citizens are bound by their common concerns and common participation in search for common solutions to common conflicts (Barber 1984, 218–219).

In Barber's democracy, citizens are regarded as legal persons, brothers, or neighbors. If they are legal persons, they are bound by a social contract and seen as both sovereign and subject by government. They have a vertical relationship to government, value accountability, and constitute one among many in the regime. If they are brothers, they are bound by blood. They constitute a corporate body and the relationship of the corporation is horizontal among citizens. Rather than valuing, most accountability emphasis is placed on fraternity. The citizen is not just one among many but is the only permissible one. If they are neighbors, they are bound by common concerns and participation. They are active participants in the affairs of the polity. They are concerned about civility and are considered first among equals (Barber 1984, 219).

In comparison, Terry Cooper builds on the work of Flathman, Mosher, Long, Salisbury, and Sniderman to construct a model of legal and ethical citizenship (Cooper 1984, 145). Cooper's primary concern is on ethical citizenship. The model is presented as a matrix which extends between high ethical and low legal types of citizenship. High legal and low ethical completes the scenario.

In Cooper's design, citizenship falls into two categories of legal and ethical divisions with four quadrants of high and low distinctions. In a high legal regime, membership is in a governmental jurisdiction with prescribed rights and obligations by law. Membership shares authority and has extensive participation by law. If the membership status is low legal as opposed to high, obligations are limited to government, authority is hierarchical, and participation is minimized by law. On the other side, if membership is high ethical, a person may belong to any community. Membership status, rights, and obligations are defined by values, norms, traditions, and customs. Authority is shared among members and participation is extensive. In contrast, if membership is low, ethical authority is hierarchical and participation is minimum (Cooper 1984, 146).

By contrast, Thomas Bryer and Sofia Prysmakova-Rivera (2018) expand Cooper's (1991), Flathman's (1981), and Lowi's (1981) legal and ethical citizenship work to construct a citizenship model with three forms: legal, political and ethical, and cultural and religious. Bryer and Prysmakova-Rivera argue that an individual does not need to be a legally recognized citizen to develop norms within the culture of a city or community in which he or she resides (Bryer and Prysmakova-Rivera 2008, 27). The model portrays the three forms of citizenship and two types of citizens (included-in and included-out).

In Bryer and Prysmakova-Rivera's scheme legal citizenship means included-in persons covered by all legal protections with obligations to abide by all laws and regulations. Those persons considered included-out in this category are persons covered by specific legal protections with obligation to abide by all laws and regulations. Under political and ethical citizenship included-in persons are encouraged to participate in candidate and issue advocacy, volunteer, and vote. Included-out persons situated here are encouraged to participate except vote and are subject to monitoring by authorities. The other category cultural and religious citizenship allows included-in persons to freely participate in accepted cultural and religious expression. Those persons included-out are free to participate in accepted cultural and religious expression with potential limitation and monitoring by authorities (Bryer and Prysmakova-Rivera 2008, 27).

Additionally, Bryer and Prysmakova-Rivera visualize these types of citizens as not being fixed in cells with immovable walls but in open circles with different shades of inclusiveness. They place the fully included person at the intersection of three interlocking circles. Included-out persons are situated at the outside perimeter of the circles. These persons are fully excluded but share public space and are either not seen or heard, or both (Bryer and Prysmakova-Rivera 2008, 28).

Citizen Equality Model Theory

I have constructed a framework for a theory of democratic citizenship that I call the "Citizen Equality Model" (CEM). This model places every citizen on equal footing. In a sense, leveling the playing field so that all may have life chances at becoming economically, politically, socially, and spiritually equal. This model locates citizen at the center and embodies him or her with economic equality (things that generate wealth), political equality (things that produce power), social equality (things that build community), and spiritual equality (things that foster peace). Full legal citizenship requires all four of these elements. Figure 8.1 illustrates the interconnectedness among the elements that constitute full legal citizenship. There is a tripartite relationship between the four dimensions. When the four domains are in equilibrium all are recessive.

What do I mean by tripartite relationship among the four domains? I mean that each of the domains interacts with one another on a regular basis through everyday routines. Each domain is distinct and dominant in its realm but crosses boundaries with one another to make society work. Actually, society would not be complete without any one of the four domains. By necessity then the domains must cooperate with one another to achieve their purposes otherwise society would malfunction.

The relationship between the four domains is triangular not square because each domain is dominant in its own space. For example, when the issue is economic, the economic domain is dominant and the other three are recessive. This creates a dominant–recessive relationship in the economic domain. If the role is switched because the issue is in one of the other domains, the

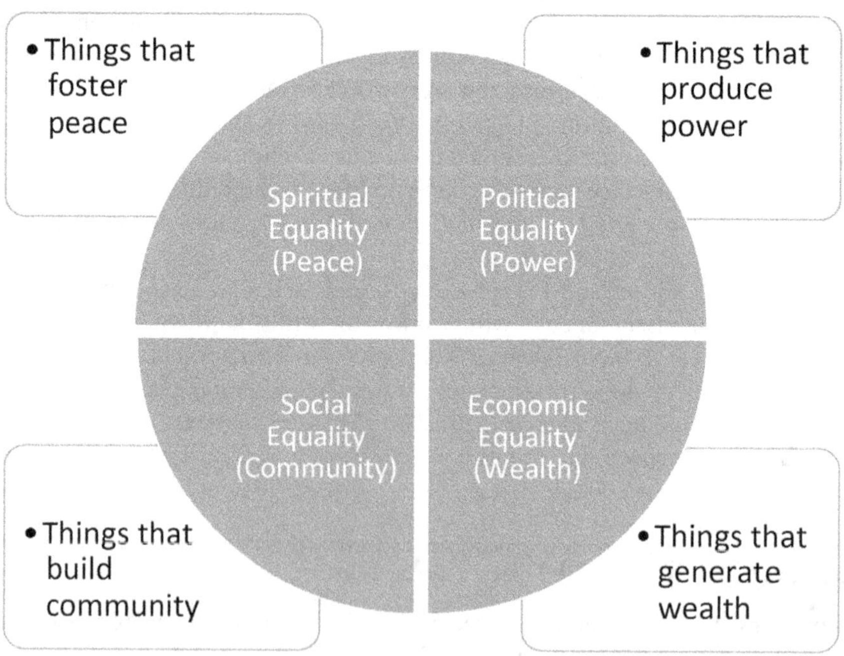

Figure 8.1 Citizen Equality Model (CEM).

dominant role becomes that which governs the issue, say political, social, or spiritual. Then the remaining three become recessive. This intercourse is reciprocal and binding to one another.

These relations are recessive to one another as each dimension is dominant in its own sphere. No citizen is abridged from exercising rights and privileges of any dimension without due process of law.

In contrast to the other models, the CEM has a legal base. This legal foundation is the social glue that holds this model together. In accordance with the Constitution, which provides "equal protection of the law," mechanisms exist to enforce all four types of equality. The other models include legal, ethical, and religious domains but not with equality in these realms. In essence, the other models lack enforcement mechanisms and leave citizens to fend for themselves. Unlike the CEM, the other models fail to address a citizen-as-a-whole person with full legal rights, privileges, duties, and immunities. They also ignore social equality. By doing so, the other models omit the problems of citizenship so prevalent in American society.

What do I mean by being a whole citizen? I mean that a citizen cannot be a full participant in society unless they possess the means to do so. What do I mean when I say that a whole citizen includes the four basic properties of equality: economic, political, social, and spiritual? I do not mean, for practical purposes, that every citizen must have the same amount but rather that every citizen must have equal opportunity to attain the equivalent in each domain. This means that no artificial roadblocks or man-made encumbrances are placed in the way as mechanisms for hindering a citizen's chances of achieving equality.

Why these four basic properties and not others? As implied above, these four properties (economic, political, social, and spiritual) are essential to the whole person. If they are the essence of a complete person then they are by necessity what embody a whole citizen. A citizen is less than others in the polity absent any one or more of these properties. No citizen is on equal plane unless full of all four properties. Equally embodied with these properties a citizen can participate fully in society and enjoy life, liberty, and the pursuit of happiness.

What do I mean by equality? I mean that all weights and balances are equivalent. In other words, there is no effective difference between two or more things. It is not a subject of morality or fairness or justice or equity—giving one what is due but possessing or transferring that which is equal. For example, a pound of pork is equivalent to a pound of beef. Or, a pound of tea is equivalent to a pound of coffee. So, it does not have to be the same, just equivalent.

What do I mean by economic equality? I mean that every citizen must have the financial means to fully participate in public life. They cannot be hindered by the everyday routines of work and other financial burdens that encumber citizen duties. They must be enabled to exercise all of their rights, immunities, and obligations afforded to them in the Constitution. They must be able to freely participate in the free enterprise system and have unrestricted access to capital and the creation of the means of production. A citizen must have opportunity to generate wealth. In other words, in a capitalistic economy, all citizens must have the economic means that enable freedom of participation to the fullest extent. If a citizen is burden by the everyday demands of earning a living, what time, resources, or interest do they have in pursuing the common wealth?

In a capitalistic economy there is economic inequality. Evidence points to growing income and wealth gap between the rich and poor. The rich getting richer and the poor getting poorer. This gap differential affects participation in all spheres of public life to the advantage of the rich and well off and often at the detriment of the poor and poorest. Those at the very bottom of the economic scale cannot fully participate in civil society at a significant rate comparable to their rich counterparts. They are priced out and moved out of high rent districts and places of prosperity and discarded as rubbish by those in the higher circles who make decisions about their well-being. In order to achieve parity, pursuit of wealth is key. The accumulation of wealth leads to parity in a capitalistic economy.

What do I mean by political equality? I mean what Dahl advocated in the sense that all or most adult citizens must have opportunity for effective participation, equality in voting, enlightened understanding, and final control of the agenda. I would add that these conditions are subject to the constraints of advanced technology; even then all are effectively equal in the same political environment—meaning every adult citizen has equal voice, vote, and participation. A citizen cannot devote proper attention to political affairs if they are not in the public sphere where their voice would be heard. Therefore, the citizen would not be heard and would have to settle for someone else to represent their interest or what is decided as majority will. How then can a citizen reduced to less than full capacity by everyday routines have an equal say or effect on public policy questions? If a citizen does not have equal political power as others in the same political environment, how can they effectively control their common destiny? What would give such a citizen the capacity to make a difference in their life and the life of their posterity? A citizen must have equality in political affairs or their citizenship status becomes less than others in a polity. A citizen must possess power.

What do I mean by social equality? I do not mean that every citizen must enjoy the same status as everyone else at the same time. However, what I do mean is that every citizen must have opportunity to rise from one social status to the highest level and not be handicapped or hindered by artificial barriers. No citizen should be barred by any arbitrary or capricious means from access to education, employment, finance, or other societal advantage that their skills and abilities entitle them. All citizens must have equal access to the highest level of social status. A citizen must become an equal part of the community. Those trapped at the bottom rung of the social ladder cannot participate fully in public life to the extent of those at the top of the ladder. They are entrapped by an array of social abnormalities. These social pathologies prevent citizens at the bottom from enjoying life, liberty, and pursuit of happiness. They are pushed and kept at the margins of society. They are stymied by the everyday occurrences or circumstances of life. Because of their low social status they are shunned, exploited, and excluded from public life. Rules and laws are established to make it difficult or discouraging for them to be productive citizens. They are ostracized, viewed with contempt, and treated as subhuman or as a noncitizen, even as society prospers and revolves around them. Many of them become victims of the criminal justice system.

A person's overall well-being is attached to the community—whether that is a community of place, memory, or a psychology. An individual cannot live alone and be socially whole. A citizen must of necessity belong to a community. It is in this context that a person participates in public life and enjoys or suffers the adventures of communal life. A community of place is the one addressed here. Etzioni argues that a community is a "web of affect-laden relationships among a group of individuals, a set of shared values, norms, and meanings, history and identity, and a relative high level of responsiveness" (Etzioni 1996, 5). Given this definition, a citizen is socialized into a whole person in the community. This citizen is then able to function appropriately in community by observing and practicing accepted norms, customs, and behaviors.

What do I mean by spiritual equality? I do not mean that all citizens have to practice the same religion or have the same spiritual beliefs or rituals. A citizen can be an atheist or agnostic. However, all citizens must have the opportunity to freely practice religion within the bounds of law. The only restraint placed on spiritual practice is conformity to the rule of law. For example, no spiritual practice would permit human sacrifice or otherwise endanger or imperil another during the course of a ritual or ceremony. A citizen must pursue peace as opposed to strife.

Those who desire to worship or practice religion must be left free to do so within the rule of law. Those who desire not to worship or practice religion must be left alone. All types of worship and religious practices must be considered equal in the eyes of government. No favoritism should be granted to one religion, unless the others enjoy the same privilege. For example, no holiday is sanctioned for one and not the other. No creed is sanctioned for one and not the other. No special status should be given to one and not the other. All worship and religious practices are equal. In this scheme, there is no separation of church and state.

SUMMARY

Historically, citizenship in America has been problematic for people of color and women. During the Colonial Period, Native American tribes were invaded and eventually pushed off their land into reservations under a series of wars and treaties. Africans and others were imported and enslaved or made indentured servants until 1863 (for Africans in rebellious states). Africans, Asians, Hispanics, and Native Americans were discriminated against and denied full citizenship until 1965. Caucasian women were similarly denied full legal citizenship until given the right to vote in 1920.

In a nation founded on *e pluribus unum*, out of many one, the full rights and immunities of citizenship in America evolved around a narrow pathway exclusive only to those privileged to become members of the club. Ironically, though the Statue of Liberty was dedicated in 1886 as a beacon of hope, democracy, and freedom, the torch in Lady Liberty's hand signified an unwelcoming message for people of color. Those others (noncitizens, undocumented, and illegal aliens) residing in the states or seeking entry were more likely to be turned away, rounded up, detained, and deported back to their country of origin.

The puzzling question is what does this history of American citizenship mean? It means that the nation has an undemocratic predisposition if a critical mass of its citizens or residents does not enjoy full legal citizenship. Further, it means that residents without full legal citizenship and those seeking citizenship and denied the same for arbitrary and capricious reasons are relegated to the shadows of civil society. If public officials enacted fair and just immigration policies, and practiced the same justly, scarce public resources would be saved and a just society would be achievable.

This peculiar history also raises the question of why certain populations are preferred over others while these other groups are denied full legal citizenship. I would surmise that, beyond appearing to be unfair and unjust, this situation may hinder the nation from becoming a more perfect union.

In order for a citizen to become whole, they must have opportunity to become economically, politically, socially, and spiritually equal. The CEM theorizes that a citizen must have equal access to wealth, power, community, and peace in a capitalistic-republic. The absence of any one of these dimensions assigns a person to less than full legal citizenship status. Partial citizenship or noncitizenship subjugates the resident to a lower status in civil society and places the nation at risk.

Chapter 9

Conclusion

Researchers have revealed that, although citizen participation has been frequently studied over the last thirty-five years, governments have not fully instituted effective or authentic participation methods. From 1984, when Cole and Caputo looked at the public hearing process, to 2009, when Woods examined public participation mechanisms, to more recent studies found in this book, public administration and communication scholars have studied how and to what extent citizens have been involved in public policymaking. Their findings suggested that citizen participation in the policymaking process has been low to moderate. The literature review suggested that there was a need for additional scholarship in the area of understanding how the public hearing process effected final public policy decisions.

Public meetings provided opportunities for citizens to achieve some of their political goals; however, this participation mechanism did not afford them opportunity for authentic participation. In some cases, citizen participation mechanisms, such as public hearings, were used as fronts to adhere to the law and to gain public endorsement of an agency's plans. Local governments frequently used participation methods but were less likely to include citizen input into the final policy decisions. Government mandates of public participation have caused public administrators to pay attention to the issue of citizen involvement. Providing more access to policymaking increased the influence that interest groups, agencies, the courts, and the governor have on rulemaking.

In general, citizens were left going through the motions with very little effect or consequence. In other words, citizens were permitted to participate in superficial ways, but they did not have much of an impact on policy decisions. It appeared that the roles of citizens and public administrators needed to be reconsidered and changed so that public input could be thoroughly interwoven into policy decisions. There seemed to be a need to rewrite obsolete citizen participation requirements for some agencies. The literature review affirmed the findings that a public hearing could be ineffective or weak as a mechanism for citizen participation in public policymaking.

Myriad issues addressed in the literature review struck at the core of democratic principles. Inherent in these principles was maintaining harmony in the administrative state while living up to the ideals of democracy. One of the primary reasons for citizen participation was for citizens' voices to be heard. This meant that the preferences of citizens would have impact on the outcome or final decision. The primary reasons why citizens approached institutions were that institutions were making policy decisions that affected them or citizens had determined that the common problem or issue could not be solved by their collective efforts alone, or perhaps institutions reached out to citizens to find solutions to public problems and issues.

Inherited and implied in the majority of studies cited above was the notion that institutions were empowered to execute public functions and that citizens might be brought into the decision-making process at a predetermined or arbitrary point of their choosing, if at all, in some cases. Implicit in this view was the notion that citizens have limited capacities to coproduce goods or services or at worse negligible contributions to make toward rulemaking and public decision-making.

However, the minority view expressed here held a counter position, essentially auguring for citizens to be included at the agenda-setting stage. This was the initial stage where the problem or issue was named and framed. In this instance, citizens would be treated as equals in identifying the problem or issue. Later stages would address the options or alternatives, the trade-offs, how the problem or issue would be solved, what resources would be used in its resolution, how citizens would collectively act, and what was learned about the situation. In essence, citizens would exercise the six democratic practices that the Kettering Foundation studies. In total, the existing research shone new light on the interconnected, overlapping, and often conflicting theories and practices of citizen participation used to work with citizens. There was no consensus on what constituted effective citizen participation and how to measure it. The studies illustrated the tension between the state and citizens in public participation.

Historically, there are at least four major challenges in the field of public administration including public versus private orientations, politics-administrative dichotomy, state and society, and interdisciplinary versus paradigm approaches. The six primary approaches to public administration are political, managerial, legal, ethical, integrated/comprehensive, and historical. The distinguishing factor separating public administration from private management is publicness. Like any field, public administration continues to evolve.

Administrative agencies have mandates to execute public functions in the United States. Because these agencies operate in a democratic environment, they have obligations to consider such as affected citizens' opinions and recommendations. Granted, these agencies have timelines and limited resources and therefore are not sitting on their hands waiting for citizen involvement. However, public administrators in charge of these agencies should be mindful that they are public servants and that their primary loyalty should be to the people and to the Constitution under which they as administrators serve.

The administration is a particularly powerful agenda-setter, as are such prominent members of Congress as the party leaders and key committee chairs. The same could be said about the governor, his cabinet, and the state legislature. Consequently, some citizens may argue that politicians, career bureaucrats, media, and experts shape policy formation, alternatives, and implementation methods. As a result, there is a disconnection between citizens and policymakers. Citizen participation and engagement should be integral parts in guiding policy analysts in evaluating policy options. Public policy affects us all in every facet of our lives whether we realize it or not. Putting citizens into the mix of policymakers is a formidable but necessary task.

In regard to public decision-making, there may be times when it is prudent to exercise a top-down approach and on other occasions a bottom-up method would be appropriate. Other times, mixed approaches may be the appropriate course of action. And during times of crisis, it may be better for the common good to allow a small group of public officials at the highest levels of government to make critical decisions. On the other hand, absent a crisis, citizens as the highest stakeholders of government should be involved in policy decisions that impact their lives. Further, there are other alternatives to conducting business-as-usual. These approaches include citizen participation, engagement, and public deliberation as alternatives for public policy development. After all, American government was intended to be "of the people, by the people and for the people."

The case of the Arlington Park Neighborhood illustrates how democratic citizens work through public problems in their communities. Ordinary citizens named and framed public problems and found solutions. In regard to the ten case studies, it seems that public administrators realized that they have public duties to perform but that engaging citizens may not be a high priority or they may not be convinced that public participation will generate efficiency, effectiveness, economy, and equity. The New Jersey Turnpike Authority (NJTA) was created as a government-sponsored monopoly in 1948. It had power to enter into business transactions and developments other than those pertaining to roads, bridges, and tunnels. The Authority generated hundreds of millions of dollars in revenue annually. Citizens appeared to have little influence over its business affairs, but were affected by its policy decisions. Using the 2008 NJTA highway toll policy initiative as an example, this study analyzed the level of citizen involvement and what effect citizens had on the final policy decision. Archival data from the 2008 public hearings (4) and a ten-day public comment period were analyzed using a qualitative content analysis methodology. Robert Dahl's theory of democratic process was used to measure effectiveness of NJTA citizen participation efforts. The results suggested that citizens were not effectively engaged in the toll policymaking processes. However, their participation influenced policy, though inconsequential, as reflected in the final policy decision adopted by the NJTA.

The cases shed light on the difficulty of pinpointing the democratic nature of how citizens shape and control their collective future. Surely, a few cases illuminated citizens engaging institutions in democratic ways. Citizens were involved in prescribed activities by attending meetings and discussions, making suggestions and deciding on problems and issues. However, it was quite difficult to ascertain the quality and effectiveness of the use of democratic practices. Given what we know about the history of citizen participation in the United States, we should not be surprised by mixed reviews regarding its success. In many cases, the prescriptions handed down by federal government have not cured the problems targeted or achieved the desired effects. Nevertheless, each generation produced its own remedies for a cure of the current strain of citizen disengagement. There is a long history of citizen participation in the United States resulting in mixed commitment and results.

Perhaps, it may be naïve to think that a populous can be found in advanced technological society practicing direct democracy. Also, a single study is similar to a photograph in the sense that it only captures a very small period of time. Therefore, it may be wise to conduct a longitudinal study on a particular city, town, or community to discover the democratic practices of which community members are engaged.

In any event, citizens are placed at a great disadvantage in postmodern society such as the United States in terms of power dynamics. The skills and knowledge that citizens possess are often not valued or are viewed as insufficient by the public officials who make decisions affecting their daily lives. Again, the meta question to raise is, how should this power dynamic be balanced?

If the end of state is justice, then all persons residing in the state are equal and citizenship is granted to all who desire it. Further, since justice and equality prevail in a state, historical wrongs perpetrated against a class of people should be compensated through a theory of reparation such as the one discussed in this book. Finally, four interwoven themes running through this book and the political climate of which it is situated are as follows: Who is a citizen? What constitutes a citizen? How are citizens controlling their common future? What is the appropriate role of government in relations to citizens? Hence, a framework for a new theory of citizenship was presented, the Citizenship Equality Model, as a construct for understanding the constitutive qualities required for full legal citizenship. A primary hypothesis for this model is, if a person possesses economic, political, social, and spiritual equality, inequities of all kinds would be substantially reduced or eliminated.

Chapter 10

Afterthoughts

Governing With *the People*

David Mathews

These are not ordinary times. People have lost confidence in our governing institutions, most notably government, especially at the federal level where I once worked as secretary of the U.S. Department of Health, Education, and Welfare (HEW). I was a bureaucrat and HEW was a colossal bureaucracy with a budget larger than all but the budgets of the United States and Soviet Union (Califano 1981, 19). Even more worrisome, many people, especially the young, are losing confidence in democracy itself. Americans would have to come together to counter these trends but the country is being hit with a tidal wave of divisiveness. Some of these troubling trends like the loss of confidence in government go back to the 1960s, so the situation is not likely to change soon.

What are the implications of these trends for public administration? I do not think that business-as-usual is going to be an adequate response. Democracy is in serious trouble worldwide. The situation we are in now makes me think of Woodrow Wilson's concern about the inevitable tension between an expert, professional administration, and democracy. That tension seems likely to grow in today's political environment.

The Kettering Foundation, a research institution not a grantmaker, has been studying how democracy might work as it should for over forty years, and we have taken Wilson's concern to heart. I will confess up front that we do not have an adequate response. But in this chapter, I will describe another way of thinking about the relationship between the citizenry and governing institutions that might open doors to discovering a more positive relationship.

Governing institutions, which includes nongovernmental organizations (such as foundations, civic associations, and educational institutions), have mounted numerous efforts to counter the loss of confidence, like public participation and accountability initiatives. But these have not stopped the erosion, and some studies suggest they have been counterproductive (Cook 1996, 134–135). Something more has to be done to counter the destructive forces at work.

There may be other strategies for dealing with the public's alienation that need to be tested. One possibility is captured in the simple title of a forthcoming Kettering Foundation Press book—*With*. The book offers another way of thinking about the relationship between The People and the governing institutions. A *with* strategy's mission is to foster a reciprocal, collaborative, mutually beneficial relationship between a democratic citizenry and its institutions: citizens do what they do best in tandem with what institutions do best. The strategy draws its inspiration from Abraham Lincoln's ideal of a government *of*, *by*, and *for* the people. Today, do Americans think our government is really "of" the people? That's debatable. "By" the people? Doubtful. "For" the people? Perhaps for some, sometimes. So why not add another preposition—more governing institutions working *with* the people?

A *with* strategy is not a set of best practices to emulate. I want to emphasize that it is just a different way of thinking about a relationship with citizens that might help in imagining new ways for governing institutions to gain more from citizens and for citizens to gain more from the institutions. During my time at HEW, I encountered specific cases in policymaking (on issues ranging from school busing to recombinant DNA) where a *with* strategy could have been useful and also conditions that made this collaboration impossible (Mathews forthcoming).

WITH AS DEMOCRACY

A *with* strategy is a democratic strategy. Saying that demands an explanation of what is meant by *democracy*, because the word has many meanings. Today, the most common definition is that democracy is a system of contested elections resulting in a representative government. Or it is a system of institutions, both governmental and nongovernmental, that serve the public. Those are certainly valid definitions. However, there is reason to believe that a democracy is much more.

I think what we now call democracy began long before the word was coined. It grew out of lessons taken from the collective actions needed for human survival when our ancestors were hunter-gatherers living in tribal enclaves. This was before there were kingdoms and nation-states. As humans spread out across the globe, they carried with them a "political DNA" developed in the struggle to survive. A principal lesson was that cooperation is key; we needed collective efforts to stay alive. We had to work *with* one another, even those from different tribes.

Much, much later, the Greeks captured some of this survival legacy in their language with new terms like *democracy*. This word has two roots: *demos*, "the people collectively," as in a village or *deme*; and *kratos*, "sovereign power," the capacity to act in a way that makes a real difference (Beekes 2010, 325, 772; Liddell and Scott 1968, 386–387, 992). Modern representative government still rests on this earlier foundation of collective decision-making leading to collective actions for collective well-being.

From this perspective, democracy began and continues as a political system in which, at the most fundamental or organic level, citizens must work with other citizens to create things—"public goods"—that make life better for everyone. Our ancestors went on to form governments and other governing institutions to create more and different goods. These two political systems, one governmental or institutional and the other organic or civic, are interdependent in the ecosystem of democracy, which is the subject of an earlier book, *The Ecology of Democracy*, from the Kettering Foundation Press. Unfortunately, this essential, symbiotic relationship becomes weaker if citizens do not join forces to produce public goods, or if they delegate much of what they must do to governing institutions. And the relationship also weakens if it is dominated by professional expertise and bureaucratic routines. These push citizens to the sidelines.

A *with* strategy is idealistic, yet it is not a pie-in-the-sky fantasy. The United States recognized the need for what citizens provide by enacting laws allowing tax exemptions for nongovernmental institutions serving public purposes (Arnsberger 2008, 106, 124). Public-institutional collaboration is, in fact, very common in some situations. Think about communities hit by natural disasters—fires, floods, and tornadoes. Before first responders or official help arrives, people rush to help one another—even those who may be strangers—possibly putting themselves in harm's way. While collaboration between citizens working together and governing agencies does occur in extreme circumstances, it is not a well-established policy with broad applications.

What Is Not Being Proposed

To avoid misunderstanding, I want to point outsome well-known and useful practices that are not what I mean by "*with*." This strategy, for instance, is not just another form of public participation. It goes beyond conferring with citizens who are beneficiaries of government programs. It is not consultative democracy. At the federal level, "with" does not mean just partnering with state and local governments. And it is not the same as transferring government responsibilities to nongovernmental organizations; it is not devolution. Neither is the strategy using volunteers to serve governing institutions, valuable as that is. And it is not the same as the partnerships that governments have with businesses and other institutions. I am not critical of any of these efforts, yet I believe there is more to be done.

Reciprocity and Complementary Production

"Working *with*" is a reciprocal relationship. The best metaphor I have for this may be too dated to mean much today. Where I am from, pine trees grow so rapidly that they are treated as a crop like corn. Seedlings are planted in neat rows so the trees can be harvested easily by machines. Before this equipment was available, the trees were cut using long crosscut saws, with two workers reciprocating in pulling the saw back and forth. Their efforts produced a result that neither laborer could have achieved by working alone. They worked *with* each other.

A *with* strategy fosters reciprocity between what citizens do on their end of the saw and what governing institutions do at their end. The strategy is based on evidence that institutions cannot do their jobs effectively without the complementary efforts of people working with people (Ostrom 1993, 8). That is because there are some things that can only be done by citizens or that are best done by them. Even when citizens and governing institutions do the same thing, like rescuing disaster victims, the fact that the rescues are done by other people builds social capital. I realize that saying there are some things only citizens working with one another can accomplish invites pushback and I will say more about that later.

The case for complementary efforts was made persuasively in Elinor Ostrom's Nobel Prize-winning research on what she termed "coproduction." Citizens cannot be left on the sidelines, she said, because their work is needed to reinforce and complete the work of governments, schools, and other institutions. Here is Ostrom's argument:

> If one presumes that teachers produce education, police produce safety, doctors and nurses produce health, and social workers produce effective households, the focus of attention is on how to professionalize the public service. Obviously, skilled teachers, police officers, medical personnel, and social workers are essential to the development of better public services. Ignoring the important role of children, families, support groups, neighborhood organizations, and churches in the production of these services means, however, that only a portion of the inputs to these processes are taken into account in the way that policy makers think about these problems. The term "client" is used more and more frequently to refer to those who should be viewed as essential co-producers of their own education, safety, health, and communities. A client is the name for a passive role. Being a co-producer makes one an active partner. (Ostrom 1993, 8)

Products from the work of citizens can complete what institutions do because civic work is different from the work of institutions. I have in mind supplementary projects that make use of people doing the things professionals do not—and cannot—do. That is why I prefer the term *complementary production* rather than *coproduction*.

A good example of complementary production is captured in a story a colleague told me about an exchange between a group of citizens in her community and their local government. The citizens had started a cultural project, but when they met with municipal officials, they did not ask them to take over the project. They simply said, "Here is what we have done, now what can you do?" People had taken the initiative, which is an important characteristic of a *with* strategy. Town officials then offered assistance using resources that the citizens did not have. That type of reciprocity is at the heart of a *with* strategy. Citizens take an initiative; they work together to make things (public goods). Then the government adds the resources it has. Collaborating *with* one another is mutually beneficial.

Citizens as Agents

I realize that many people reading what I've said about citizens are pushing back because they doubt that citizens are likely or able to do their share of the work a *with* strategy requires. And their reservations are not without reason. The greatest challenge to a *with* strategy has to do with the way citizens see themselves, act, and are seen by others. Americans have not just lost confidence in governing institutions, they sometimes lack confidence in one another. What is more challenging is that if people are to be coproducers, they have to make things, both tangible and intangible. This concept of citizens as producers is novel because, even in participatory projects, citizens are more often seen as constituents to be heard or consumers of government services. They do not necessarily make anything by working with others.

There are many abilities and resources people have that allow them to do their share of the work with governing institutions (Mathews forthcoming). I will discuss one of these capabilities here because it has to do with a common criticism of people, which is that they are too ill-informed and biased to be effective citizens.

A Faculty for Sound Judgment

Of course, collectively we can be foolish and wrongheaded. And even though we have innate abilities, it does not mean that we will use them. But that recognized, human beings have survived for eons because our ancestors made, more times than not, the kind of decisions that allowed them to avoid extinction. Most ancient languages have words for the kind of decision-making that leads to sound judgments. In English, the word *deliberation* is taken from Latin and it means to weigh the value of something as on an old-fashioned balance scale.

Given the variety of meanings of deliberation today, it is no wonder that there is some confusion about the kind that is needed in a *with* strategy. One misperception is that deliberation is an almost magical process or technique. Not so. Neither is deliberation just civil and informed conversation or discussion. It is hard choice work that requires grappling with tensions among differing options for action. And public deliberation seldom or ever results in full agreement on solutions. However, genuine deliberations can show a range of actions that people will or would not take or support, which allows them to move forward in combating a problem. Deliberation shows what is practical, what most people can "live with."

In a nutshell, public deliberation begins in deciding how to describe an issue in terms of what people consider deeply valuable—their security, their freedoms, being treated fairly. Then, various options for dealing with the problem, options that reflect what people hold dear, have to be crafted. What needs to be done? Who should act? Once the major options are on the table, decision-making begins in order to find out what people will and would not do. That is difficult because the things people hold dear may be in tension with one another. What is done to give greater security may infringe on people's freedom to act as they wish. Such tensions have to be recognized and worked through, not to reach perfect agreement (which is not likely) but to the point that people recognize what they are and are not willing to do as they face a troubling issue. Locating the politically permissible allows them to move forward.

Are people too apathetic to deliberate? They are not if the deliberations are rooted in what people consider deeply valuable and hold dear. At issue in nearly every issue is what is deeply valuable to people. I do not mean "values," I mean the ends and means of life itself (Rokeach and Rokeach 1989). There are many things people hold dear that lie at the deepest level of human motivation. These are ancient imperatives I just mentioned—security, control, freedom, and fairness. They are important to everyone.

As deliberations go on, in the best cases, initial, hasty reactions become more reflective and shared judgments. Participants in deliberations can not only develop a better understanding of issues, but alsothe tough trade-offs that have to be made. And they can gain a better understanding of others, even those with whom they continue to disagree. "You are wrong but, given what you experienced, I can understand why you hold such a mistaken opinion." This understanding can change the tone of a conversation. It becomes less toxic. Realizing that the tensions are among things that are valuable to everyone helps change the decision-making from one of people against people to people against a common problem.

Although everyone has the same primal concern about their well-being, people live under different conditions, so they put different priorities on what they hold dear. Because of their circumstances, people in one community may consider safety more important than some personal freedoms. Yet, living under other circumstances, the priorities in another community may be reversed.

Because circumstances can vary a great deal, deliberation requires giving a "fair trial" even to options that some may have reason to oppose. Admittedly, recognizing what is good in an option labeled as bad is a challenge. Although it is tempting to avoid what could be an unpleasant conversation, it is imperative to have opposing views and recognize the inevitable tensions among all that people hold dear. These tensions cannot be resolved by no longer caring about things that are deeply valuable, so people have to find a way to balance or harmonize competing concerns. That is what deliberative decision-making encourages.

Public deliberation is crucial in dealing with public issues that require public judgment. We have to use our best judgment when faced with decisions that have no certain technological or scientific answers. There are a number of possible answers, and we have to select the ones that fit with the things we consider essential to our well-being.

This kind of deliberation is a natural act, not a special technique to be learned and copied. Our brains are organized to deliberate. In their review of the neurobiology of decision-making, Ernst and Paulus explain how deliberative decision-making is integrated into the neurological process (Ernst and Paulus 2005). In scientific terms, deliberation is closely associated with the functions of the right dorsolateral cortex and the orbitofrontal cortex. Other parts of the brain contribute emotional processing, which is critical in deliberation.

The elements of deliberation can be heard everywhere. Go to a coffee shop or bar; people talk about problems that concern them, about what action should be taken to respond, and about who needs to act. These casual conversations may not sound deliberative, yet deliberation is not something apart from ordinary speech. Formally organized deliberative forums help people to prompt more deliberation everywhere decisions are made.

For over thirty years, on a wide range of difficult issues, my colleagues and I at Kettering have seen people trying to deliberate, even on very controversial issues. Sometimes these efforts have failed but enough have not for us to recognize this faculty exists. These deliberations are called National Issues Forums (NIF). Today, NIF deliberations are sponsored by an array of organizations around the country—even by prisons. These organizations see the forums as serving their institutional missions, not as simply as an one-time project.

When deliberation is recognized for its importance, and public meetings provide opportunities for people to move beyond complaining, wish listing, and just discussing issues to deliberative choice making, people have the opportunity to become more effective citizens. Deciding together paves the way to acting together to create public goods, and this process instills a sense of ownership and responsibility.

Public Deliberation and Governing Institutions

Clearly, the professionals in governing institutions cannot do the work of citizens for them. However, public administrators can help create the conditions that can facilitate collaboration. And they can avoid doing things that make a *with* strategy less likely. An example is being open to and encouraging citizens to try to make the tough decisions the country and their communities face.

An experiment in Hawaii showed the potential for this kind of collaborative exchange on a controversial issue, allowing gambling in a tourist paradise. The experiment had implications for both unelected and elected officials. Added revenue from gambling was attractive; the fear of crime and corruption was not. In this case, legislative leaders worked with faculty at the University of Hawaii to organize deliberative forums (Foley 2006; Ihara 2003). The purpose of the forums was not to tell the legislature how to vote, it was for legislators to see how people were thinking when they had to think, in order to weigh the trade-offs (Ihara 2003). Nongovernmental institutions can also benefit from hearing the public deliberate on the issues they care about.

Resources Citizens Can Draw On

A particularly daunting criticism of citizens is that even if they can deliberate, they do not have the resources to do what they have decided needs to be done. In reality, citizens do have unique resources (Mathews forthcoming). For example, institutions like hospitals can care *for* people but family and friends can care *about* them. (We now have evidence of how powerful a medicine that caring can be.) And citizens can supply the local knowledge that comes from living in a place 365 days a year. Using this knowledge, people understand how to do things that are different from what professionals do. Human caring and local knowledge are powerful resources, which are often underutilized.

Another resource that people can draw on is their ability to form associations at the grassroots level. That was evident in a 2018 study of what has allowed some cities to lower their crime rates when others could not (Sharkey 2018). Researchers found that "every 10 additional [civic] organizations in a city with 100,000 residents . . . led to a 9 percent drop in the murder rate and a 6 percent drop in violent crime" (Badger 2017). These associations did not necessarily regard their work as preventing violence, but "in creating playgrounds, they enabled parents to better monitor their children. In connecting neighbors, they improved the capacity of residents to control their streets. In forming after-school programs, they offered alternatives to crime" (Badger 2017). Even if not directly related to crime, these efforts helped turn negative emotions into positive energy.

Differences in Ways of Working

Some of the most powerful resources available to citizens come from their distinctive ways of working, which are different from those of institutions and can complement them. Why are there differences? After all, the tasks that make up any kind of work are similar. Most all work involves identifying problems, making decisions about what needs to be done, finding the necessary resources, organizing the efforts, and evaluating what happens; nothing exceptional about that.

However, the way citizens go about these tasks democratically is different. The differences begin in things as basic as how problems are described or "named." People do not identify problems using the expert language common to professionals in governing institutions. Citizens tell stories about the things that they hold most dear: security, freedom, and being treated fairly. The things held dear motivate people to act and that motivation can be more powerful than institutional prohibitions and inducements. Citizens' options for actions to solve problems also go beyond the things that can be done by institutions, such as actions by families and the civic associations people form. The resources citizens can also draw on to implement their decisions, like personal talents and experience, are different from institutional resources. And citizens organize their work less bureaucratically than institutions. They can also evaluate results differently using the things they hold valuable as standards rather than just quantitative measures.

Unfortunately, civic and institutional ways of working may not only fail to mesh with the work of citizens, but have adverse effects on what people do. For example, citizens typically work through small, informal, grassroots associations. These groups are quite unlike highly structured governing institutions. When large institutions try to work with these citizens' groups because they are good at what they do, the institutions may unintentionally remake them in their own image or "colonize" them. The result is that the citizens' groups lose their identity as authentic agents of the people, which is what makes them effective.

Engaging Governing Institutions

To propose any kind of change in what institutions do, like working more *with* the citizenry, it is useful to have some grounding in how a governing institution actually functions. At the federal level, the agencies in the executive branch are in the best position to collaborate with civic organizations and citizens. They are staffed by able public servants who work in large bureaucracies, which are necessary given the scope and complexity of the programs they direct. Bureaucratization, however, brings with it certain mind-sets and values that can be problematic for a citizen-centered *with* strategy. While inevitable, these obstacles are not insurmountable.

Large bureaucracies, nongovernmental as well as governmental, tend to "see like a state" and may not be as aware of local conditions and human concerns as citizens are, so they appear to lack "common sense" (Scott 1999). They are charged with enforcing rules uniformly and, in doing that, may not take into consideration extenuating circumstances. Even before enforcement, creating the rules without sufficient opportunities for the general public to weigh in will alienate people. Adding to the alienation, rules are legalistic, and that can create a climate not conducive to collaboration between citizens and governing institutions. (These obstacles are not because of "bumbling bureaucrats." It should be noted that public criticism of this sort does not work.) Bureaucracies function the way they do for valid reasons, given their missions and purposes. The work of citizens has to be better aligned with what bureaucracies do.

A BETTER ALIGNMENT

Kettering research suggests that governing institutions and the citizenry can work effectively together by realigning their efforts so that they are mutually reinforcing. The way citizens go about their work has to be recognized in the way that institutions do theirs. The challenge, as I have said, is that these two ways of working are not the same and can be seriously misaligned. As noted, citizens and institutions alike give names to problems, but the terms are not identical. Yet it should not be too difficult for officials to recognize the names people use in their descriptions of issues. Officials also have to respect, not just recognize, the way people see problems. When officials do, alignment is possible. Of course, people's experiences and the names that grow out of what people experience can be misleading. Still, officials benefit from starting where people start. A better alignment between citizens and institutional actors does not necessarily require officials and professionals to do a great deal more but rather to do what they are already doing a bit differently.

Ideally, governing institutions and associations of citizens will collaborate for their mutual benefit. The Hawaii case is an example of what can happen when there has been a sharing of deliberations. As officials deliberate among themselves, they have to weigh various policy options against their costs and consequences. They have to consider tensions among the things they consider valuable as they weigh pros and cons. This is their "choice work." Citizens do the same thing, albeit in their own terms, when they deliberate. When officials sit down with deliberative citizens to compare the outcomes of their respective efforts at choice work, they are aligning*with* one another. And that has actually happened at the federal as well as the state level (Neblo et al. 2018). (Municipal institutions should take note.)

Office holders can benefit from hearing a deliberative public because it is a voice different from those that officials are attuned to hearing. It is not the voice of polls or focus groups, of constituents, or even of interest groups. A deliberative voice can tell them how citizens go about making up their minds when there are costs and other trade-offs to consider. Legislators and public administrators cannot create this citizens' voice, yet they can help create a climate where such a voice is likely to develop. When citizens have deliberated in forums on an issue that is also before the government, for instance, the outcomes of the public deliberations have been helpful to elected representatives by showing them routes they can take that are less likely to lead to polarization. Exchanges between legislative bodies and a deliberative citizenry are excellent examples of a *with* strategy at work.

Recently, members of Congress have been in an experiment using online deliberation to listen to citizens. The results were reported in a 2018 book titled *Politics with the People*. It shows the potential to help counter the loss of public confidence when government authorities (legislators) join citizens in the work of deliberation (Neblo et al. 2018). Michael Neblo, one of the authors, noted the positive results of exchanges that allow elected officials to hear citizens engaged in "thoughtful deliberation" in online forums (Neblo 2009). This experiment involved thirteen sitting members of Congress who were dissatisfied with the often acrimonious and unproductive town meetings, but recognized their duty to consult with their constituents. Using a new online deliberative town hall technology developed for NIF, both the citizens and the representatives behaved differently in what proved to be a "more satisfying and constructive" experience (Neblo et al. 2018, 5). Hopefully these deliberative exchanges will spread to more state legislatures as well. They reflect democratic values like openness and reflective judgment, which are the defining characteristics of a *with* strategy.

I would add that there is another benefit for this kind of exchange. Assemblies, from city councils to state houses to the federal Congress, must be deliberative bodies if they are to remain legitimate in the public's eye.

THEN AND NOW

Now, as always, the most hotly contested issue is whether Americans are able to meet the responsibilities of citizenship. As you have read, I think that there are ways for citizens to make some of the differences in the political system that they would like to make. But I do not have any doubt-eradicating proof. That acknowledged, and also recognizing that people collectively have acted foolishly and worse at times, democracies have, nonetheless, endured because of a faith in The People. I am reminded of one of the first tests of that democratic faith, which occurred at the onset of the American Revolution. Would the people in the colonies support a war against one of the world's superpowers, Great Britain? Daniel Webster recalled that founders like John Adams had responded to the doubters unequivocally by insisting that citizens were not fickle but would stay the course in the resistance to British aggression. Perhaps influenced by his own era's democratic spirit in 1826, Webster imagined Adams rising to rhetorical heights to capture the spirit of 1776: "But we shall not fail. The cause will raise up armies; the cause will create navies. The people, the people, if we are true to them, will carry us, and will carry themselves, gloriously, through this struggle" (Webster 1826, 40–41). This was the same citizenry that Abraham Lincoln placed his faith in at Gettysburg.

IMPLICATIONS FOR PUBLIC ADMINISTRATION?

Does public administration today have Adams' faith in the citizenry or share Lincoln's vision of a government of, by, and for The People? The jury seems to be out. Tina Nabatchi, who teaches democracy and public administration at Syracuse University, has doubts about the tension that Wilson recognized is being reduced. She is alarmed by talk about the "deconstruction of the administrative state." She fears a "growing democratic rollback" and calls for new thinking in public administration. However, she finds the field "reluctant (perhaps incapable) of responding in a meaningful way." Her evidence includes the failure of the accrediting agency for public administration (ASPA) to even mention democracy in its standards (Nabatchi 2019).

I am more hopeful. My reason is that the threat to democracy is so great that it will challenge public-administration-as-usual to change. Will that mean using the idea of a *with* strategy? I am not sure. The changes might move in a different direction, which could be fine. But necessity is the mother of invention, and I believe there are inventive professionals in public administration.

Appendix A

Community Development and Birmingham, Alabama

Birmingham, Alabama, is a southern city with a rich industrial history and a legacy of social strife and isolation. Interviews were conducted with two city planners and one Department of Housing and Urban Development (HUD) community builder. In 1974, under a directive from HUD to involve citizens in community development, Birmingham organized itself into ninety neighborhoods. The HUD area director's letter to the mayor, in part, stated that no later than January 1, 1974, the city will have developed, under direct city control, the functional capacity to involve its citizens directly in the community development process (LaMonte 1995). In 1974, with major input from black citizens, Birmingham produced a comprehensive neighborhood-based citizen participation program for community development (Wilson 2000). Today, Birmingham has ninety-nine neighborhoods and elected officers representing the neighborhoods.

METHODOLOGY

Interviews were conducted with the director of planning, engineering, and permits and the director of community development for Birmingham by the author in 2004. An interview was also conducted with a HUD community builder, operating out of Birmingham. The purpose of this chapter was to ascertain how community planning and development professionals view community development, citizen participation and engagement, and to discover what drives community development. The interviews were audio-taped and range from thirty to forty-five minutes. A set of questions was prepared for each interview. Each interviewee was allowed several minutes to review the questions at the start of the interview. All interviewees were informed that other questions might arise during the course of the interview. This report is limited by design as it consists of only three interviews. This chapter sheds light on the subject and provides impetus for further research. The following section contains excerpts from interviews conducted for this report.

INTERVIEWS

The first interview is with the director of planning, engineering, and permits for the City of Birmingham.

How Are Citizens Involved in Your Work?

All kinds of ways on a regulatory level, we have citizens who are appointed to serve on the many boards and agencies that we bring projects before for review. Planning Commission, the subcommittees of the Planning Commission, the Zoning Board of Adjustments, the Design Review Committee, and the Historical Commission. We also work with most of the committees through neighborhood associations. Before a project goes on the agenda in the district, it is brought before the neighborhood for approval. There is an aspect of citizens letting us know what they need through the budgetary hearing processes, the City Council meetings, phone calls, and neighborhood association meetings. Our process has a demand-driven aspect to it. Citizens are the ones who really articulate those needs.

Do You Find That Citizens Understand the Nature of Your Work? What They Would Like to See Done in Their Communities and the City?

I think that they understand very much the nature of what they would like to see done. The nature of what we do and how we do it often depends on how well we communicate to them.

How Are Your Projects Demand Driven?

They are largely demand driven. There are times when we have a different kind of demand. We may have a regulatory imposition placed upon us by a court, by a federal mandate, a requirement associated with funding that we have to respond to as well. . . . But much of what we do, look at the bond programs, the capital programs in general, they are things that the citizens say they wanted.

How Do You Prioritize Projects?

That's done through any number of ways. Certainly, working with the Mayor's Office. Working with neighborhoods—getting a sense of technical urgency. Doing a cost/benefit (analysis, for example) to see whether handling a project dealing with storm sewer flooding takes priority over a project that may be with a sidewalk or some other project.

How Does Economics Factor into Project Development, in Terms of, Corporate Interests versus Citizen Interests?

It's not always versus. A lot of times we find out there is more common interests than not. People want to have a quality environment where they are located. So, that's a good thing whether you are a citizen or CEO. . . . In the final analysis, I think this is where everybody wants to get. I don't really know in our arena that we frame our conversation so it's one versus the other. I think it's really trying to provide attention to citizens across the board within the constraints that we have of resources and so forth. . . . The stabilizer of all of this is good economics. You need a good residential base, a good business base. So, the best way for us to do that is to keep the lines of communications open and bring everybody in. . . . So, it's really about getting folks to the table. But, most important for everybody—no matter what—is they want to be heard. They want to know that if they get involved—it's going to mean something—it's just not a burn on their time.

Do All Citizens Have an Equal "Say" in Project Development in Birmingham?

I'll tell you this. The best that I can answer that question is from knowledge of how other cities operate. Birmingham, through its neighborhood association—particularly provides a fantastic forum to help make sure that happens. More than many other cities I've seen—that you got a neighborhood association that is the real unit of government.

Do You Find That Certain Sections of the City Have More Political Power than Others?

No. I haven't found that—just from a sense of canvassing the area. I'll tell you this without hesitation that when that phone rings and no matter whom it may be—if it's a citizen with an issue they are heard the same way. It absolutely matters not. . . . If the basic question is one of access and audience—that is about as even across the board as I have seen it anywhere. . . . There are a lot of things that go into making a project in a timely way. Resources outside of

City Hall are just as important as resources inside. If you go to cities where things are moving, you have to leverage both sides—public and private.

How Do Citizens Representing Distressed Communities Get Projects Done?

Through neighborhood associations, through coming to City Hall and letting us know what it is they need and how seriously they need it. To us working with them and getting other agencies—like the federal government and state government to help us. . . . All of us as cities look to the states and feds to help us financially. Getting those resources in is often what's needed in some of those areas that are referred to as "distressed." Whether you are dealing with housing through CDBG (Community Development Block Grants) or flood mitigation through FEMA (Federal Emergency Management Agency), the Corps (Corps of Engineers), or whatever, the city has to be a strong advocate for federal partnership.

What Is Your Assessment of Community Leadership in This Area?

Well, I have very good interface, more in terms of the substance of it, than with any style, with the citizen leaders that I have been involved—both the neighborhood association and the community advisory board. One of the nice things about Birmingham is that over the years with the citizen participation program, you have citizens who are used to gaining access to their government. There is an institutional sense that "hey, we are here" and that we need to be listened to. . . . It's fascinating for me to look across the city and see the kind of leadership that's put forward. I mean the kind from each different neighborhood. When they come together like at a citizens advisory board level—to talk about what's going on and try to move things forward. I think it's a very fine system. My interface with the neighborhood leadership on an individual basis has been very good. . . . For the most part I've been impressed with the caliber of people that come up through the system. It's interesting because many of the elected officials we have were grown through that process as well. It's really been an incubator for a lot of the elected leadership in the city.

What Is Really Driving Development in This Area? Is It More Economics or Community?

I think to some extent, those are false choices. It may be where I am that I see the connections. You really cannot part those and not expect some impact on the other. You got to work them together. . . . You really have to think about community that has economics in it as a component rather than it being one or the other. If there is anything absolutely abrasive to me it's a community concept. Almost everything you do in a community will have an economic impact. . . . I guess what I'm saying that it always concerns me when I hear either questions or constructs put together that would inherently place those at odds. . . . I really think it's a false argument to try and make this thing too polemic. What you got to do in a public arena like a city or county or whatever is really try and get the interests served toward the greatest good across the board. I've never seen any developer in the final analysis, even when you have a project that's got a good community benefit, go in and accept a bad deal.

The second interview is with the director of community development for the City of Birmingham.

What are some of Your General Thoughts on Community Development?

My mentor here was the former director of planning, engineering and permits. He had the spirit that the way to get work done in neighborhoods was to engage everybody in the conversation. Get everybody around the table and talk through it. He transmitted to me the sense that everybody had ideas of value and that an open democratic conversation can get you to closure. A lot of people are scared of doing that. If you are scared of it, you tend to close people off and try to channel conversations and talk to key players and not have that broad-based community conversation. He believed that the more ideas you get at the table, the better off your decision is going to be. But one of the things that I struggle with right now is a real disconnect. I think you really have to be precise about language, between citizen participation and real citizen ownership of development, of economic development, of housing problems, of neighborhood revitalization. . . . We seem to be stuck in a mindset of citizen participation—involved in conversations and neighborhoods are left looking to City Hall to fix their problems. Rather than them having the means and wherewithal and support to get out there and do it. When the community development program came online in the early to mid-seventies, the city was required to have a citizen participation program as part of their HUD program.

We formed a citizens participation program that was staffed out of City Hall. We had a community resource staff for that program. We elected neighborhood officers. We have now ninety-nine neighborhoods. Every two years we have neighborhood elections. It's a very democratic organization. The city allocates $10,000 a year (per neighborhood) to the neighborhoods to do certain projects. In many ways it's a very democratic structure. But, those associations have not been allowed to incorporate. They've been told that they can't use the funding as seed money to do other projects.

In a way, in the name of democracy and citizen participation, we've created something that is very democratic and very participatory, but we've put a cap on it. And said OK you can do only these kinds of things. And it has somewhat thwarted the "hell raisers." It sort of thwarted the folks who might have organized a nonprofit around an issue and raised hell with City Hall. It sort of made the neighborhoods, in a way, creatures of city government. And, to some extent, kept the lid on moving to that next level of becoming the agent of change in the neighborhood. So, it's almost like we are stuck in time. We are stuck at that level of having open conversations, democratic processes, and all of this exchange of information.

What Are Residents of the Ninety-Nine Neighborhoods Doing? Are They Channeling Their Ideas About Change or Needs?

Theoretically, they are but again we have recent experience. The (City) Council has been asking about how many folks participate in (neighborhood meetings). We've got 240,000 people in the city. We did a count over a three-month period about how many folks are active—showing up to meetings. There were a little over 2,000 people citywide from these 99 neighborhoods. So, we are getting right at 1 percent. Again, while it has a democratic structure, it's not engaging large portions of the community. Its open and its accessible, but it isn't really reaching large numbers of folk.

How Do You Go about the Community Planning Process? Who Is Involved in the Process? What Are You Trying to Accomplish?

It's been different things at different points in time. And it's really in the process of changing right now too. It used to be about every ten years we'd do a series of documents called "needs assessments documents." Like we had a mid-seventies generation, a mid-eighties generation of needs assessment done neighborhood by neighborhood. They were mainly statistical profiles and inventories of conditions in neighborhoods. The most interactive process we've done—I guess about four or five years ago—we started working with individual neighborhoods. . . . We did neighborhood development plans. Working interactively with the neighborhoods. That's about a six to eight month process. It followed a model borrowed from "assets-based community development approach." We met every other month with a group from the neighborhood. It was very much participatory. They set the goals. They decided what their priorities were. And the plans reflected their goals and priorities. . . . That involved only three neighborhoods though. We didn't do the whole city. And again, part of it is that we don't have the manpower to do those citywide.

How Does the City Determine Where to Allocate Its Resources? Are There Phases? Does the City Rank Communities?

We have not gotten into ranking. . . . We really are doing two things. One is there are areas where we have done detail planning . . . and we are trying to implement those plans. That's sort of an intentional act on the part of the city—say that we think neighborhoods can come back and are important to bring back. So, we are intentionally going in neighborhoods and trying to bring in builders. What we are doing has multiple phases—it's a balancing act because we don't have unlimited resources. We can't commit $200 million. We get about $10 million a year from HUD's CDBG and Home Program. Plus we get some program income. All total we have about $14 million to work with from the federal government for neighborhood revitalization. We get a little bit of bond money—about $3 million that the city puts up in bond funds. . . . So, what we are trying to do is strike a balance of going into target neighborhoods and finding a block or two where we can go in and build a dozen houses and maybe repair another dozen houses in a limited couple of blocks. Put up new street lights, fix broken sidewalks and kind of make a statement in a very small limited area. . . . The reason it got to be limited is because if we try to do a twelve or fifteen block area, we don't have the resources to do that in ninety-nine neighborhoods. Plus, we don't know if the market will support it.

Do You Sense That Economics Drives Community Development?

Absolutely, the reality of it is that there is not enough resources in government to fix these neighborhoods. . . . In Birmingham, everybody knows the history—the sixties—you had a lot of people leaving the city as fast as they could. You had houses going up for sale. It's basic economics 101. . . . You got more of whatever commodity—be it widgets or houses . . . on the market than you have buyers—so prices go down. . . . So you had white flight during the sixties and seventies. We lost about 25,000 residents in a couple of decades. . . . Over 20,000 every decade in the past four decades. The first two decades were mainly white flight. In the last two decades, most of the white folks were already gone, so we lost a lot of the black middle class. . . . There are all sorts of vacant houses. There is not a realtor working in some of these neighborhoods because there are just not buyers in a lot of the neighborhoods. So, our theory is you got to fix the economics. . . . You see more vacant storefronts than occupied storefronts. It just sends all of the wrong messages to the market. So, the city doesn't have the resources to fix it all. What we hope to do is be a catalyst in sending new messages.

What Is Your Concept of Community?

My concept of community is very historical. I was listening to an elderly lady . . . she started talking about when she was a little girl—she just described her neighborhood. She said we didn't have any money. We lived in a little "shotgun house." But then she said that across the ditch was where the doctor lived. She named the doctor and said that he had a very big nice house. . . . She said that her teacher lived on the corner of the block. There was a store down the street. . . . I really think that that's what we have lost. We have segregated ourselves in this country by income. You know the rich folks live outside the city and the poor folk live in Birmingham. It's not ironclad that that holds true. . . . To me, that's where we have lost a sense of community. In having a place where the doctor, the teacher, and the maid can all live together. We don't have that any more—at least, not in Birmingham.

What Are Your Thoughts on Community Building?

Community building is about putting information and resources back into the hands of the grassroots people—and not controlling. . . . I think you have to accept that community building has to be at times contentious. That's what we missed in Birmingham. We don't have that edge to the dialogue. There is never contentiousness of community people advocating for their community. Being at odds with City Hall—because I think that we have just kept a little more control on it than there should be for it to be a healthy community.

How Do You Characterize Community Leaders That You Come in Contact with in Birmingham?

Wow! There is not a single profile. In a lot of ways certain of them are somewhat controlling. To the extent, some of the neighborhood presidents are president for life. They've been president for twenty years. So, it's expected that they are going to be reelected president. It's somewhat of a power trip, somewhat of a control thing. And we got other folks—a younger group wanting to do things but are frustrated. They look for how to pull the right rings at City Hall to make the "money tree" drop money on them. I don't see any of them out there really pulling an organization together. There are attempts to do that—they try to leap rather than try and organize around—let's fix one house. They try to leap to become housing developers. . . . The mind-set is more what are the magic buttons to push in City Hall to get things fixed by city government. If I could change one thing, it would be that. I would love to be able to have a group of neighborhood leaders who were out there taking ownership and responsibility.

The final interview is with a HUD community builder, located in Birmingham.

What Is a Community Builder?

Our initial charge was to be aggressive in various communities in Alabama. Try to build up communities. Try to identify needs, address needs, that sort of thing. . . . At the time, it was considered fairly unique. Community fellows would be aggressive in the community as opposed to allowing people just to come to us or call us for something. We would go out into the community and solicit—actually act as marketing representatives . . . to sell our wares. To convince the community that, indeed, we could help. We were able to do that very aggressively in ways that had not been done before. Just get up and do presentations as to how to go about accessing what we have to offer. . . . Four hundred people were hired at the national level. We had about seven or eight in Alabama. They were assigned to a state by congressional districts.

What Does Building up Communities Mean?

Primarily focus on areas of community development—economic development—jobs. For example, the Black Belt, education, economic, and social needs—we would go in and try to pull together community leaders to try and prioritize what the issues were . . . try to match or leverage federal dollars with private and public dollars within a community to address a specific concern.

What about Citizen Involvement in Your Work?

As a matter of fact, in order to qualify for a federal program, you have to show evidence of citizen involvement. We are shifting from a needs-based approach to an asset-based approach. I always tell people that everybody has needs even in a wealthy community. . . . You have to identify your assets and what you are bringing to the table to match any kind of federal grant. . . . Selma would be a good example. Over a six-month period, we conducted a series of seminars.

Identifying what the needs are, meeting once or twice per month, and identifying a cross-section of the community. . . . We developed a white paper out of that and used that white paper to go after federal grants and to attract partnerships with the public and private sectors. This partnership resulted into a $750,000 project to address housing, education and job training.

What Would Poor People in the Black Belt Have, in Terms of Assets, to Bring to the Table?

Well, social networks, social glue, religious affiliation—identifying what that is in a community can leverage federal funds. To me a consensus around a need within a community helps us to leverage federal funds and attract private dollars-in-kind or real dollars.

Why Is HUD Interested in Community Development?

Part of what we are charged with is to try and upgrade communities, address needs using federal dollars to attract private-sector local dollars to address construction needs—capital needs . . . job training, unemployment, housing stock—that sort of thing is part of our national goals.

Do You Think HUD Is Really Making a Difference in Community Development?

I think so. We have spent quite a few dollars—billions of dollars and millions of dollars in this state. The way it works, you got to have matching funds. The funds we put out are not going to solve all of the problems in Alabama. So, what we have to do . . . is leverage those dollars. Sometimes two or three to one match in private-public local dollars.

Has HUD Ever Considered Training Citizens to Become Community Leaders?

Well, hopefully going through the partnership—the process of applying for grants—leaders will emerge from all sectors. They become more knowledgeable about what can be done. People float to the surface that ordinarily would not think of being able to make things happen. So, in a practical sense as opposed to a formal sense, leaders develop over time.

How Does HUD Prioritize the Allocation of Its Resources?

We have national goals. Within the national goals, whatever the specific needs are in a community would dictate what . . . their priorities are.

How Would You Characterize the State of Affairs of Community Development in Alabama?

I would say it's sort of uneven. Some are doing very well. Higher level than others—primarily, it's education, job training, and job rates driving some of that. The Black Belt has always been a challenge . . . education, skill level, job training, employment rates have to be addressed in order to have even development across the state. From central to north Alabama has always done better than central to south Alabama.

What Explains the Unevenness That You Cite?

A lot of it is political—historic; a lot of it is education—density of population. Education has not been a priority. Over time people have out migrated—better educated people . . . the big urban areas have attracted people from small rural areas. So, that leaves a big hole in terms of employment, education levels, interests, and community leadership.

IMPLICATIONS FOR FURTHER STUDY

As this research indicates, community planners and community development professionals proclaim citizen involvement in their work, and that the community development work has shifted from a needs-based to an assets-based approach. The extent of citizen involvement could not be determined by this research. I sense that a mix of economic and community interests drives community development activities. However, the interviews raise some important questions. Do economic interests outweigh community interests? Or, are they inseparable? Are there projects where community interests dominate economic interests? Or vice versa? Are community interests often dominated by economic interests? Are community development projects executed in a democratic fashion? Is it usually a win-win situation for citizens and other parties? Who really decides what's in the best interest of the community? Do citizens have the capacity to represent their interests? These questions provide impetus for further research.

SUMMARY

This chapter focused on Birmingham, Alabama, a southern city with a rich industrial heritage and a legacy of social strife and isolation. In 1974, Birmingham was directed by HUD to involve citizens in the community development process. The result was the creation of a citizen participation program eventually evolving into ninety-nine neighborhoods with citizen representation. Interviews were conducted with three community planners and community development professions to get their take on community development. Although this research raised as many questions as it answered, it addressed some of the issues associated with community development: limited resources, housing, jobs, education, neighborhood revitalization, economics, partnerships, and citizen participation. The effectiveness of the citizen participation program has mixed reviews. Economic interests and community interests may not always be polar opposites but partners. The true value of these interviews may lie in their resourcefulness for further study.

REFERENCES

LaMonte, E. S. 1975. *Politics and Welfare in Birmingham, 1900-1975.*The University of Alabama Press.

Wilson, B.M. 2000. *Race and Place in Birmingham: The Civil Rights and Neighborhood Movements.* Rowman and Littlefield Publishers, Inc.

Appendix B

An Annotated Bibliography

The methodological approach of public administration I chose is the political approach. The primary reason I selected this approach is that it views public administrative issues as policymaking, power struggle, and resource allocation among different groups (Lan and Anders 2000). I was particularly interested in policymaking as it may indicate the level and effect of citizen participation.

This bibliography was organized thematically under four headings: political origins, reinventing government, public management, and public administration. Each of these themes provides a perspective on the development of public administration and the role of politics as its central core. These perspectives shed light on major theories, ideas, concepts, and controversies in the field of public administration.

POLITICAL ORIGINS

Argyle, N.J. 2002. "Developing a Foundation: Administration in the Polis." *Public Administration Quarterly* 26: 346–372.

The author argues that the foundation of Western administrative structures exists in the Greek city-state. The Greeks are credited with developing many governing structures and concepts about political philosophy. This study focuses on these administrative structures and examines the political thoughts supporting them. More specific, it focuses on the contributions of Socrates, Plato, and Aristotle. In regard to an organizing framework, the author explores their views of man and society. The author posits that the first view might be labeled individualistic and the latter communal. Further, the author asserts that this framework can be subdivided into four cells: marketplace, protectorate, responsive commonwealth, and directed commonwealth. Generally, the author concludes that students of public administration can learn much from the study of the Greek city-state. The West remains heavily influenced by ancient Greece.

Dunsire, A. 1999. "Then and Now Public Administration, 1953-1999." *Political Studies* 47: 360–378.

This article provides a British perspective on the development of public administration. The author states that since 1953 the field and subject have undergone major changes: "permanent revolution," "culture shift," "new paradigm," or have gone from "traditional public administration" to "new public management," or "governance." The author presents a personal overview of the subject and field of public administration. He refers to the "field" as the real-world activity—the creation and delivery of public services and structures and people through which it is done. The "subject" as defined by the author is the academic study of public administration both teaching and scholarly research based mainly in universities and colleges. The author states that the field in 1953 comprised the description and system. It was not grasped holistically as a creed much less a conceptual model. It was taught toward degree or diploma in only a few universities by a scattering of lone specialists. The author argues that the field began to change during World War II. He asserts that four developments occurred during the period of 1953–1975 that reshaped the landscape of public administration. These changes are the drive for corporate management and planning in local government, the institutional explosion in higher education following the Robbins Report in 1963, founding of the Social Science Research Council in 1965, and the election of Margaret Thatcher as leader of the Conservative Party in 1975.

Guy, M.E. 2003. "Ties that Bind: The Link between Public Administration and Political Science." *The Journal of Politics* 65: 641–655.

The author argues that a century ago the two fields of political science and public administration were one. During the 1939 meeting of the American Political Science Association, public administration created its own professional organization, and the two fields' paths have since diverged. This article outlines the divergence, parallel paths, and convergence that link these fields. Methods and models of inquiry are discussed as they affect the influence of the fields on civil society. The author recants the intent of Woodrow Wilson's essay "The Study of Administration" as a vision of administration untouched by politics. The author cites contributions by Frank Goodnow and Leonard White in this same vein. In tracing the history of political science, the author notes the *Political Science Quarterly* as the first journal of the field in 1886; by early 1900s, courses began appearing on college campuses, and the Brookings Institute was created. The author asserts that the intellectual heritage of public administration, entwined in the development of political science, resulted from a conceptualization of politics that trusted science and technology more than popular will. The author concludes by stating that making political science without adding public administration is like making bricks without straw.

REINVENTING GOVERNMENT

deLeon, L., and R. B. Denhardt. 2000. "The Political Theory of Reinvention." *Public Administration Review* 60: 89–97.

In this article, the author examines the implications of the reinvention movement. The primary premise of the reinvention movement is that the accumulation of the narrowly defined self-interests of many individuals can equal public interest. In regard to the market model, the reinvention movement argues that government should not only adopt the techniques of business administration, but adopt its values as well. Among these, business values are competition, social choice, and entrepreneurial spirit. The author asserts that the market model implies that participants can serve the public interest simply by concentrating on their own self-interest. The author posits that the reinvention movement also emphasizes customer-driven government. Further, the author asserts that the reinvention movement prefers a government that responds to the short-term self-interests of customers rather than supporting the public interests of citizens. The third element of the reinvention movement is the idea of entrepreneurship. This notion suggests that government agents should act on self-interest or that of the agency. In conclusion, the author admonishes that as we respond to the reinvention movement or any other fad, we must understand that we are rejecting or accepting a particular viewpoint. We are making political theory.

Fox, C. J. 1996. "Reinventing Government as Postmodern Symbolic Politics." *Public Administration Review* 56: 256–262.

In this article, the author argues that much of the reinventing government can be understood not as substantive reform but as symbolic politics of a particular postmodern kind. The author posits that the reinvention of government is not what it appears to be to public administrators trapped in the logic of modernism. Scholars in public administration have delineated the internal contradictions of the reinvention movement. The author posits that a rhetorical orientation known as postmodernism has swept through universities over the last decade and may aid in understanding the reinvention movement. In other words, the work and study of public policy formation and implementation now occur in a context so fundamentally different from the past to justify the judgment that we have crossed over from modernity to postmodernity.

Rosenbloom, D.H. 1993. "Editorial: Have an Administrative Rx? Don't Forget the Politics!" *Public Administrative Review* 53: 503–507.

The author argues that recommendations for ad ministrative reforms at the federal level inevitably involve issues of separation of powers and the distribution of burdens and benefits in the polity. Calling for "management impact statements" is insufficient. We need a full-fledged discussion of the political impact of the would-be reformers' prescriptions. A look at the historical record shows that if we buy into significant administrative reform, then we are also buying into significant political change. The author argues that the idea that public administration can be separated from politics is odd. It was not present at the founding, but later became the cornerstone of public administration orthodoxy. It continues to define a good deal of administrative thought, including "entrepreneurial government in which 'steering' is conceptually separated from 'rowing.'" The author asserts that the civil service reformers of the 1870s and 1880s developed the politics-administration dichotomy. It was installed in American government by the Progressive movement. Further, the idea that governmental administration could and should be apolitical was widely opposed by entrenched politicians and their followers. Opponents wondered how apolitical administration could be responsive to the people and be representative.

The political power struggle underlying the politics-administration dichotomy has been largely ignored or somewhat misunderstood in mainstream public administrative thought.

The dichotomy was a weapon in a monumental struggle between "two thoroughly different systems of political ethics." In conclusion, the author posits that in the zeal to promote visions of the public interest, American administrative reformers sometimes seek to remake the political system to serve the needs of better management rather than to develop better management to serve the purposes of the political system. Administrative theory is political theory and administrative prescription is political prescription. This is an old lesson: if we want better government, we better talk politics.

PUBLIC MANAGEMENT

Felts, A.A., and P. H. Jos. 2000. "Time and Space: The Origins and Implications of the New Public Management." *Administrative Theory & Praxis* 22: 519–533.

The authors argue that the rise of the new public management inspired by market models has startled the field of public administration. This article explains the swift rise of the theory and practice of the new public management by exploring the economic, cultural, and epistemological roots of capitalism, the authors assert. Further, the authors argue that reinvention, downsizing, entrepreneurial risk-taking, and contracting out have produced dramatic changes in government agencies. In addition, the authors posit that the speed and scale of both the academic and institutional advance of the new public management is even more disconcerting since it represents a serious challenge to many of public administration's commitments to values. The authors pose the question, why now? The authors assert that the answer begins by remembering that public organizations are rooted in capitalism. They conclude by stating that organizing inquiry around the dichotomy of public/private leaves the field vulnerable to exaggerating both the wisdom of bureaucratic procedures and the capacity and willingness of public administrators to engage the public.

Johnston, J., and G. Callender. 2000. "Multiple Perspectives on Economic Rationalism and the New Managerialism: Power and Public Interest?" *Administrative Theory & Praxis* 22: 585–604.

The authors argue that the economic rationalist, new managerialism (ERNM) paradigm of public management, based on neoclassical economics is promoted as offering potential benefits for all. It could be argued that adoption of an ERNM-directed framework by government favors power elites at the expense of the rest of the community. In this environment, the rhetoric of wider opportunity may be used simply for electoral purposes to persuade the polity that there is some egalitarian benefit from adherence to such a paradigm. The authors posit that another interpretation suggests that political elites have been unwittingly persuaded by rhetoric of business and intellectual neoliberalists to develop strategic public governance frameworks that favor them. The third possibility is that altruism has motivated elites who are acting in the interests of all the polity. In this article, the first and second possibilities are the basis of an examination of the extent to which power is a critical influence on contemporary government policy and administrative action.

Stivers, C. 2000. "Resisting the Ascendancy of Public Management: Normative Theory and Public Administration." *Administrative Theory & Praxis* 22: 10–23.

The author argues that though the field of public administration has historically been grounded in tension between a science-based quest for efficiency and essentially contested questions that mark public life, this conceptual arena is sieged by adherents of public management, who reject "traditional" public administration in the way Herbert Simon did more than fifty years ago.

Taking Dwight Waldo's position that public administration is fundamentally a theory of politics, this article argues that while scientific knowledge has a place in the field, the quest for a science of management should not be permitted to occlude the political. The author argues that normative theory points us in the direction of usable knowledge, a form that is neither pure science nor conventional wisdom, and concludes by suggesting a stance for normative theorists, one aimed at preserving the publicness of public administration. The author posits that if public management were to succeed in its quest, transformation of the field into a science, the result would no longer be public administration (or, for that matter, public management).

"Public" does more than describe the kinds of agencies we study; it represents the constitutively contestable dimensions of our subject matter. Further, normative and critical theory—public administration understood as political theory—is the indispensable source of publicness in the field of public administration. The author asserts that this is the site of resistance to the notion that public administration can ever be, in any uncomplicated sense, a science. After outlining this argument, the article concludes with suggestions about the stance normative theorists might adopt in order to preserve the publicness of public administration.

PUBLIC ADMINISTRATION

Lan, Z., and K. K. Anders. 2000. "A Paradigmatic View of Contemporary Public Administration Research. An Empirical Test." *Administration & Society* 32: 138–165.

This article offers an empirical articulation of paradigmatic views that guide research in contemporary public administration. Based on the findings, the authors argue that the debate on whether there is an intellectual core in public administration is becoming less relevant. What is more important from this point on is public administration scholars' self-consciousness and better articulation of these existing paradigms. A self-aware normal science practice in public administration offers us a clearer research focus, a sharper sensitivity for recognizing anomalies, and thus a better chance for advancing public administration theories. The authors assert that for decades public administration scholars have engaged themselves in discourses of various kinds to search for an intellectual core for the field. Further, they state some scholars are still troubled by the thought that there is no viable, broad-ranging paradigm to govern public administration research and to replace scientific management and the politics-administration dichotomy. Public administration has never stopped being a developing field since its first inception as an independent academic program in 1926 at Syracuse University.

The authors conclude by stating that the study has augmented the empirical literature describing the status of public administration research by offering a paradigmatic framework to help public administrators evaluate the field. The findings of this study have revealed a set of tacitly agreed-upon paradigms that guide public administration research. The foremost governing paradigm is publicness. In addition, the authors identified six subparadigms: political approach, managerial approach, judicial approach, ethical approach, integrated/comprehensive approach, and historical approach.

Lowi, T.J. 1993. "Legitimizing Public Administration: A Disturbed Dissent." *Public Administration Review* 53: 261–264.

The author argues that efforts to legitimize public administration go back a long way. In the past decade or so, these efforts have turned toward legitimizing public administration as a separately constituted institution of government. Further, legitimizing public administration is something every regime has to do. The Federalists probably saw administration legitimized as long as "a few good men" were in place to make a few good decisions. The Jacksonians had a theory of legitimate administration that was, in fact, a general theory of government within which administration was legitimized. In effect, government should not only be small within a strict construction of the constitution, it should never be involved in any activity that is beyond the ability of the common person to administer. The author argues further that meritocracy was the late nineteenth-century, middle-class answer to the highly successful legitimizing theories of the Jacksonian democracy.

The neutral civil servant was the key to legitimacy, not the professionalism by itself. This made meritocracy logically compatible with legislative supremacy, which is the core of the American constitution. Through the nineteenth century and well into the twentieth century, several theories were aimed at legitimizing public administration. The purpose was to flesh out a more general ideology or theory of state more consonant with the party or regime in power. In conclusion the author posits that of all the preceding efforts to legitimize public administration, the current effort most resembles the original Federalist approach. Conservatism has emerged and coalesces around an effort to provide America with a new approach to public administration as the core of a new, more conservative regime.

Luton, L.S.2002. "The Tale That Wagged the Dog: Is the Progressive Era the Foundation of American Public Administration?" *Administrative Theory & Praxis* 24: 439–456.

The author argues that the Progressive Era is not the foundation of American public administration. Granting the significance of that era in framing a self-conscious, professional public administration in the United States, it argues that the importance of the Progressive Era has been overstated. The author prefers to depict that era's contributions as part of a series of framings and reframings of American public administration. The article does that by: (1) recognizing some of the key themes of the Progressive Era; (2) identifying some of the key themes of eras before and after the Progressive Era; and (3) suggesting how all of the contributions of the various eras ought to be recognized in order to properly understand how twenty-first-century American public administration came to be and how it might evolve.

The author further posits that the treatment of the management movement and the Progressive Era as representing the time period when professional public administration began to take shape includes an admission that the century between the constitutional founding and the civil service reform movement provided the soil in which the seed of professional public administration took root. The point of the article is not to denigrate the contributions of the Progressive Era, but to depict them as part of a series of framings of public administration, not its founding.

CONCLUSION

In conclusion, the author posits that there have been many framings of American public administration. The Progressive Era is not the foundation for American public administration. Non-Progressive themes are found in both Pre-Progressive and Post-Progressive thought and practices. In three periods, American public administrators have attempted to deal with complex and vexing questions regarding appropriate approaches to democratic public administration. There is no one best way to approach public administration, only ways that are better (or more poorly) suited to the expectations and values of a given time.

There appears to be uncertainty as to the origins of public administration. Some scholars argue that it began during the Progressive Era. Others assert that it began long before then even as far back as ancient Greece. However, many scholars generally agree that the field of public administration appears to have undergone a metamorphosis around World War II. It was around this time that the field broke away from political science.

There is also general agreement that the field underwent major changes in 1953—from "traditional" public administration to new public management. Some scholars are skeptical and troubled by the new public management approach and question the motives behind this movement. Still others are searching for an intellectual core for the field. In any event, most scholars would agree that the field of public administration has a political origin and that publicness distinguishes it from private management.

References

ACT Alliance. 2011. *Shrinking Political Space of Civil Society Action*. http://www.actalliance.org/resources/publications/Shrinking-political-space-of-civil-society-action.pdf.

Adams, B. 2004. "Public Meetings and the Democratic Process." *Public Administration Review* 64(1): 43–54. doi:10.1111/j.1540-6210.2004.00345.x.

Alexander, M. 2012. *The New Jim Crow. Mass Incarceration in the Age of Color Blindness*. New York, NY: The New Press.

Anderson, J. E. 2006. *Public Policymaking: An Introduction*.6th ed. Boston, MA: Houghton Mifflin.

Anduiza, E. P. 2002. "Individual Characteristics, Institutional Incentives and Electoral Abstention in Western Europe." *European Journal of Political Research* 41.

Argyle, N. J. 2002."Developing a Foundation: Administration in the Polis." *Public Administration Quarterly* 26: 346–372.

Arlington Park Neighborhood Minutes: November 23, 2003; January 11, 2004; February 15, 2004; March 21, 2004; April 18, 2004; June 20, 2004; August 15, 2004; September 19, 2004.

Arlington West End Neighborhood Improvement Plan. 2002. City of Birmingham.

Arnstein, S. R. 1969. "A Ladder of Citizen Participation." *Journal of the American Instituteof Planners* 35(4): 216–224.

Barber, B. 1984. *Strong Democracy: Participatory Politics for a New Age*. Berkeley, CA: University of California Press.

Barbieri Jr., W. A. 1998. *Ethics of Citizenship: Immigration and Group Rights in Germany*. Durham, NC: Duke University Press.

Barker, D. W. M. 2009. *Tragedy and Citizenship: Conflict, Reconciliation, and Democracyfrom Haemon to Hegel*. Albany, NY: State University of New York Press.

Beierle, T. C., and D. M. Konisky. 2000. "Values, Conflict, and Trust in Participatory Environmental Planning." *Journal of Policy Analysis and Management* 19(4): 587–602. doi:10.1002/1520-6688(200023).

Bertram, C., and Q. Hoare. Eds., Trans. 2012. *Of the Social Contract and Other Political Writings*. New York, NY: Penguin Books.

Birkland, T. A. 2005. *An Introduction to the Policy Process. Themes, Concepts, and Models of Public Policymaking*. 2nd ed. Armonk, NY: M. E. Sharpe.

Blessett, B. 2016. *Citizenship: An Exploration of Its Meaning and Impact for Returning Citizens, Their Families and Communities.* Unpublished report. Dayton, OH: Kettering Foundation.

Boyte, H. 1984. *The Backyard Revolution: Understanding the New Citizen Movement.* Philadelphia, PA: Temple University Press.

Bramson, R. A. 2005. "Involving the Public in Economic Development." *Economic Development Journal* 4(3): 24–31.

Brody, S. D., D. R. Godschalk, and R. J. Burby. 2003. "Mandating Citizen Participation in Plan Making: Six Strategic Planning Choices." *Journal of the American Planning Association* 69(3): 245–264. doi:10.1080/01944360308978018.

Bruun, E., and J. Crosby. 1999. *Our Nation's Archives. The History of the United States in Documents.* New York, NY: Black Dog & Leventhal.

Bryer, T. A., and S. Prysmakova-Rivera. 2018. *Poor Participation. Fighting the Wars on Poverty and Impoverished Citizenship.* New York, NY: Lexington Books.

Bull, M. 2017. *Safe Routes to School: Using Parent Dialogue to Reframe and Prioritize.* Unpublished report. Dayton, OH: Kettering Foundation.

Cohen, M., and N. Fermon. 1996. *Princeton Readings in Political Thought.* Princeton, NJ: Princeton University Press.

Cole, R. L., and D. A. Caputo. 1984. "The Public Hearing as an Effective Citizen Participation Mechanism: A Case Study of the General Revenue Sharing Program."*American Political Science Review* 78(2): 404–416. doi:10.2307/1963372.

Constitution of the United States (as amended).

Cook, B. J. 1998. "Politics, Political Leadership and Public Management." *Public Administration Review* 58(3): 225–230.

Cook, T. E. 2005. *Governing with the News: The News Media as a Political Institution.* Chicago, IL: University of Chicago Press.

Cooper, T. A. 1984. "Citizenship and Professionalism in Public Administration." *Public Administration Review* 44: 143–149.

Cornford, F. M. 1972. *The Republic of Plato.* New York, NY: Oxford University Press.

Crenson, M. A., and B. Ginsberg. 2004. *Downsizing Democracy: How America Sidelined Its Citizens and Privatized Its Public.* Baltimore and London: Johns Hopkins University Press.

Dahl, R. A. 1998. *On Democracy.* New Haven, CT: Yale University Press.

Dahl, R. A. 2003. *How Democratic Is the American Constitution?* 2nd ed. New Haven, CT: Yale University Press.

deLeon, L., and R. B. Denhardt. 2000. "Thc Political Theory of Reinvention." *Public Administration Review* 60: 89–97.

Dubois, W. E. B. 1962. *Black Reconstruction in America: 1860–1880.* New York, NY: Atheneum.

Dudley, L., N. Gniady-Banford, and K. Webb-Farley. 2016. *Public Participation in Six Federal Agencies: An Examination of Public Officials' Perceptions.* Unpublished report. Dayton, OH: Kettering Foundation.

Dudley, L., M. Leighninger, and N. Gniady. 2014. *Four Federal Agencies Collaboration with the Public.* Unpublished report. Dayton, OH: Kettering Foundation.

Dunsire, A. 1999."Then and Now Public Administration, 1953–1999." *Political Studies* 47: 360–378.

Etzioni, A. 1995. *Rights and the Common Good.* New York, NY: St. Martin's Press.

Etzioni, A. 1996. "The Responsive Community: A Communitarian Perspective." *American Sociological Review* 61(1): 1–11.

Fagotto, E., and A. Fung. 2009. *Sustaining Public Engagement: Embedded Deliberation in Local Communities.* Everyday Democracy and Kettering Foundation.

Fahrmeir, A. 2007. *Citizenship: The Rise and Fall of a Modern Concept.* New Haven, CT: Yale University Press.

Felts, A. A., and P. H. Jos. 2000."Time and Space: The Origins and Implications of the New Public Management." *Administrative Theory & Praxis* 22: 519–533.

Fine, G. A., and B. Harrington. 2004. "Tiny Publics: Small Groups and Civil Society." *Sociological Theory* 22(3): 341–356.

Fox, C. J. 1996. "Reinventing Government as Postmodern Symbolic Politics." *Public Administration Review* 56: 256–262.

Gaynor, T. 2015. *Street Knowledge: Residents as Experts in Global American City.* Unpublished report. Dayton, OH: Kettering Foundation.

Girvetz, H. K. 1967. *Democracy and Elitism. Two Essays and Selected Readings.* New York, NY: Charles Scribner's Sons.

Guy, M. E. 2003. "Ties That Bind: The Link Between Public Administration and Political Science." *The Journal of Politics* 65: 641–655.

Hajnal, Z., and P. G. Lewis. 2003. "Municipal Institutions and Voter Turnout in Local Elections." *Urban Affairs Review* 38(5): 645–668.

Hale, Mike. 2005. Sheriff, Jefferson County, Alabama. Interview by author January 27, 2005.

Halvorsen, K. E. 2003. "Assessing the Effects of Public Participation." *Public Administration Review* 63(5): 535–543. doi:10.1111/j.1540-6210.2009.01997.x.

Hamlett, P. W., and M. D. Cobb. 2006. "Potential Solutions to Public Deliberation Problems: Structured Deliberations and Polarization Cascades." *Policy Studies Journal* 34(4): 629–648. doi:10.1111/j.1541-0072.2006.00195.x.

Held, D. 2006. *Models of Democracy.* 3rd ed. Stanford, CA: Stanford University Press.

Horiuchi, Y. 2005. *Institutions, Incentives and Electoral Participation in Japan. Cross-Level and Cross-National Perspectives.* London, UK: Routledge Curzon.

Hudson, W. E. 2006. *American Democracy in Peril. Eight Challenges to America's Future.* 5th ed. Washington, DC: CQ Press.

Hyman, D. N. 2005. *Public Finance: A Contemporary Application of Theory to Policy.* 8th ed. United States: Mason, OH: Thompson.

Isin, E. F. 2002. *Being Political: Genealogies of Citizenship*. Minneapolis, MN: University of Minnesota Press.

Isin, E. F., and B. S. Turner. 2007. "Investigating Citizenship: An Agenda for Citizenship Studies." *Citizenship Studies* 11(1): 5–17.

Janoski, T. 1998. *Citizenship and Civil Society: A Framework of Rights and Obligations in Liberal Traditional, and Social Democratic Regimes*. Cambridge, UK: Cambridge University Press.

Johnson, Pete. 2005. Presiding Judge, Criminal Division of District Court, Jefferson County, Alabama. Interview by author January 26, 2005.

Johnston, J., and G. Callender. 2000. "Multiple Perspectives on Economic Rationalism and the New Managerialism: Power and Public Interest?" *Administrative Theory & Praxis* 22: 585–604.

Ketcham, R. 2003. *The Anti-Federalist Papers and the Constitutional Convention Debates*. New York, NY: Penguin.

Kihl, M. R. 1985. "The Viability of Public Hearings in Transportation Planning." *Journal of Applied Behavioral Science* 21(2): 185–200. doi:10.1177/002188638502100210.

King, C. S., K. M. Feltey, and B. O. Susel. 1998. "The Question of Participation: Toward Authentic Participation in Public Administration." *Public Administration Review* 58(4): 317–326. doi:10.2307/977561.

Kingdon, J. 2003. *Agendas, Alternatives and Public Policies*. 2nd ed. New York, NY: Longman.

Knutson, E. 2014. *It's Our Turn to Decide: Participatory Budgeting in the 49th Ward*. Unpublished report. Dayton, OH: Kettering Foundation.

Koontz, T. M. 1999. "Citizen Participation: Conflicting Interests in State and National Agency Policy Making." *Social Science Journal* 36(3): 441–459. doi:10.1016/S0362-3319(99).

Kretzmann, J., and J. McKnight. 1993. *Building Communities from the Inside Out: A Path Toward Finding and Mobilizing a Community's Assets*. Chicago, IL: ACTA Publications.

Lan, Z., and K. K. Anders. 2000. "A Paradigmatic View of Contemporary Public Administration Research: An Empirical Test." *Administration & Society* 32: 138–165.

Levine, P. 2013. *We Are the Ones We Have Been Waiting For: The Promise of Civic Renewal in America*. New York, NY: Oxford Press.

Lindaman, K. 2015. *Wicked Problems, Landlords and Renters: The City of Fairborn Tackles Civic Governance Through Coproduction*. Unpublished report. Dayton, OH: Kettering Foundation.

Lindaman, K. 2017. *Transportation: City of Winona*. Unpublished report. Dayton, OH: Kettering Foundation.

Lowi, T. J. 1993. "Legitimizing Public Administration: A Disturbed Dissent." *PublicAdministration Review* 53: 261–264.

Luton, L. S. 2002. "The Tale That Wagged the Dog: Is the Progressive Era the Foundation of American Public Administration?" *Administrative Theory & Praxis* 24: 439–456.

Madison, J. 2003. Federalist Paper #51. In *The Federalist Papers* edited by G. Wills, 314–319. New York: Bantam Dell.

Martin, P. 2013. *Population Bulletin: The Global Challenge of Managing Migration.* http://www.prb.org.

Mathews, D. 1999. *Politics for People.* 2nd ed. Chicago, IL: University of Illinois Press.

Mathews, D. 2006. *Reclaiming Public Education by Reclaiming Our Democracy.* Dayton, OH: Kettering Foundation Press.

Mathews, D. 2014. *The Ecology of Democracy: Finding Ways to Have a Stronger Hand in Shaping Our Future.* Dayton, OH: Kettering Foundation Press.

Mauer, M., and R. S. King. 2007. *Uneven Justice: State Rates of Incarceration by Race and Ethnicity.* Washington, DC: The Sentencing Project.

McComas, K. A., and C. W. Scherer. 1998. "Reassessing Public Meetings as Participation in Risk Management Decisions." *Risk: Health, Safety & Environment* 9(4): 347–360.

McGinnis, M. D., and E. Ostrom, B. E. Wright. 2012. "Reflections on Vincent Ostrom, Public Administration, and Polycentricity." *Public Administration Review* 72(1): 15–25. doi:10.111/j.1540-6210.2011.02488.x.

McGregor, M. A. 2006. "When the 'Public Interest' Is Not What Interests the Public." *Communication Law & Policy* 11(2): 207–224. doi:10.1207/s15326926clp1102_2.

McKeon, R., and C. D. C. Reeve. 2001. *The Basic Works of Aristotle.* New York, NY: Random House.

Mill, John Stuart. 1996. *On Liberty and the Subjection of Women.* Edited by T. Griffith. Ware, Hertfordshire: Wordsworth Editions Limited.

Mills, C. W. 2000. *The Power Elite.* New York, NY: Oxford University Press.

Milner, H. 1997. "Electoral Systems, Integrated Institution and Turnout in Local and National Elections: Canada in Comparative Perspective." *Canadian Journal of Political Science* 30(1): 89–106.

Minor, R. C. 2004. *Higher Education, Community Building and Community Leadership.* Unpublished report. Kettering Foundation.

Minor, R. C. 2013. *Citizen Participation: A Case Study of New Jersey's 2008 Toll Policy Initiative.* Unpublished dissertation. Minneapolis, MN: Walden University.

National Assessment Government Board. 1998. *Civics Framework for the 1998 National Assessment of Education Progress.* National Issues Forums Institute. www.nifi.org.

Neuse, S. M. 1983. "From Grassroots to Citizen Participation: Where We've Beenand Where We Are Now." *Public Administration Quarterly* 7(3): 294–309.

New Jersey Turnpike Authority. 2004. *New Jersey Turnpike Regulations Relating to the New Jersey Turnpike and the Garden State Parkway, Effective.* December 9, 2004. Woodbridge, NJ: NJTA Commission.

New Jersey Turnpike Authority. 2008. *Financial Statements: Turnpike Revenue Bond Resolution Basis and Supplementary Information.* Woodbridge, NJ: Ernst & Young.

New Jersey Turnpike Authority. 2008. *Notice of Supplemental Public Hearing for a Toll Adjustment.* Woodbridge, NJ: NJTA Commission.

New Zealand Ministry of Justice, Chief Electoral Office. *New Zealand Elections Results. The Justice and Electoral Committee. Inquiry into the 2004 Local Authority Elections*. The Justice and Electoral Committee. http://www.clerk.parliament.govt.nz/Content/SelectCommitteeReports/I7C%20for%20website.pdf.

Oneil, P. H. 2007. *Essentials of Comparative Politics*. 2nd ed. New York, NY: W.W. Norton & Company.

Ostrom, E. 1996. "Crossing the Great Divide: Coproduction, Synergy, and Development." *World Development* 24(6): 1073–1087.

Patton, C. V., and D. S. Sawicki. 1993. *Basic Methods of Policy Analysis and Planning*. 2nd ed. Upper Saddle River, NJ: Prentice Hall.

Peardon, T. P. 1952. *The Second Treatise of Government by John Locke*. New York, NY: The Bobbs-Merrill Company.

Piest, O. Ed. 1957. *Utilitarianism. John Stuart Mill*. Indianapolis, IN and New York, NY: The Bobbs-Merrill Company Inc.

Putnam, R. D. 2000. *Bowling Alone: The Collapse and Revival of American Community*. New York, NY: Simon & Schuster.

Putnam, R. D. 2015. *Our Kids: The American Dream in Crisis*. New York, NY: Simon & Schuster.

Raaflaub, K. A., J. Ober, and R. W. Wallace. 2007. *Origins of Democracy in Ancient Greece*. Berkeley, CA: University of California Press.

Raelin, J. A. 2003. *Creating Leaderful Organizations: How to Bring Out the Leadership in Everyone*. San Francisco, CA: Berrett-Koehler Publishers.

Rawls, J. 1999. *A Theory of Justice*. Rev. ed. Cambridge, MA: Harvard Press.

Reich, R. B. 2007. *Supercapitalism: The Transformation of Business, Democracy, and Everyday Life*. New York, NY: Alfred A. Knopf.

Rittel, H. W. J., and M. M. Webber. 1973. "Dilemmas in a General Theory of Planning." *Policy Sciences* 4: 155–169.

Roberts, N. 1997. "Public Deliberation: An Alternative Approach to Crafting Policy and Setting Direction." *Public Administration Review* 57(2): 124–133.

Roberts, N. 2004. "Public Deliberation in an Age of Direct Citizen Participation." *America Review of Public Administration* 34: 315–353.

Robinson, C. 1983. *Black Marxism. The Making of the Black Radical Tradition*. Chapel Hill, NC: The University of North Carolina Press.

Rogers, W. W., R. D. Ward, L. R. Atkins, and W. Flynt. 1994. *Alabama. The History of a Deep South State*. Tuscaloosa, AL: The University of Alabama Press.

Rose, R. 2004. "Voter Turnout in the European Union Members Countries: Voter Turnout in Western Europe Since 1945." In *Electoral Engineering: Voting Rules and Political Behavior*, edited by Maria Gratschew and Rafael Lopez. Stockholm: International Institute for Democracy and Electoral Assistance.

Rosenbaum, W. A. 1976. "The Paradoxes of Public Participation." *Administration & Society* 8: 355–382.

Rosenbloom, D. H. 1993. "Editorial: Have an Administrative Rx? Don't Forget the Politics!" *Public Administrative Review* 53: 503–507.

Salmore, B. G., and S. A. Salmore. 2008. *New Jersey Politics and Government: The Suburbs Come of Age*. 3rd ed. New Brunswick, NJ: Rutgers University Press.

Sandel, M. J. 2009. *Justice: What's the Right Thing to Do?* New York, NY: Farrar, Straus & Giroux.

Saward, M. 2003. *Democracy, Key Concepts*. Cambridge, UK; Oxford, UK; Malden, MA: Polity Press Blackwell.

Senge, P. M. 2006. *The Fifth Discipline: The Art and Practices of the Learning Organization*. New York, NY: Doubleday.

Schneider, H. W. 1958. Ed. *Leviathan Parts I and II. Hobbes*. New York, NY: The Bobbs-Merrill Company.

Schugurensky, D., and J. P. Myers. 2003. "A Framework to Explore Lifelong Learning: The Case of Civic Education of Teachers." *International Journal of Lifelong Education* 22(4): 325–352.

Seddon, T. 2004. "Remaking Civic Formation: Toward a Learning Citizen." *London Review of Education* 2(3): 171–186.

Shafritz, J. M., and E. W. Russell. 2005. *Introducing Public Administration*. 4th ed. New York, NY: Pearson Education, Inc.

Shafritz, J. M., A .C. Hyde & S. J, Parkes. 2004. *Classics of Public Administration*. 5th ed. Belmont, CA. Thomson Wadsworth.

Silverblatt, A. 2004. "Media as Social Institution." *American Behavioural Scientist* 48(1): 35–41.

Skocpol, T. 2003. *Diminished Democracy: From Membership to Management in American Civic Life*. Norman, OK: University of Oklahoma Press.

Smith, R. M. 1985. "The Meaning of American Citizenship." American Political Science Association and American Historical Association.

Smith, R. M. 1997. *Civic Ideals: Conflicting Visions of Citizenship in U.S. History*. New Haven, CT: Yale Press.

Stansfield, C. A. 2004. *A Geography of New Jersey: The City in the Garden*. 2nd ed. New Brunswick, NJ: Rutgers University Press.

Steelman, T. A. 2001. "Elite and Participatory Policymaking: Finding Balance in a Case of National Forest Planning." *Policy Studies Journal* 29(1): 71–89. doi:10.1111/j.1541-0072.2001.tb02075.x.

Stenberg, C. W. 1972. "Citizens and the Administrative State: From Participation to Power." *Public Administration Review*: 190–198.

Stiglitz, J. E. 2016. *Rewriting the Rules of the American Economy. An Agenda for Growthand Shared Prosperity*. New York, NY: Roosevelt Institute.

Stivers, C. 2000. "Resisting the Ascendancy of Public Management: Normative Theory and Public Administration." *Administrative Theory & Praxis* 22: 10–23.

Teorell, J., M. Torcal, and J. R. Montero. 2003. "Political Participation." Paper presented at the Citizen, Involvement and Democracy Conference, Madrid, Spain.

Truman, D. B. 1971. *The Governmental Process: Political Interest and Public Opinion*. 2nd ed. New York, NY: Alfred A. Knopf.

Tsadik, H. 2015. *Engaging for Peace in Small Civil Society Space: The Role of Citizens and NGOs in Present-Day Ethiopia*. Unpublished report. Dayton, OH: Kettering Foundation.

United Nations. 1948. *United Nations Declaration on Human Rights*.

United Nations. 1985. *United Nations Declaration on Human Rights of Individuals Who Are Not Nationals of the Country in Which They Live.*

United Nations News Centre. 2012. *Restrictions on NGOs Worldwide Undermining Human Rights.* http://www.un.org/apps/news/story.asp?NewsID=41858.

Verba, S., K. L. Schlozman, and H. E. Brady. 1995. *Voice and Equality: Civic Voluntarism in American Politics.* Cambridge, MA: Harvard University Press.

Warburton, N. 2001. *Philosophy: The Classics.* London and New York, NY: Routledge.

Warren, Mark E. 2004. "What Can Democratic Participation Mean Today?" In *Representation and Democratic Theory.* Edited by David Laycock. Vancouver, Canada: UBC Press.

Webler, T., and S. Tuler. 2006. "Four Perspectives on Public Participation Process in Environmental Assessment and Decision Making: Combined Results from 10 Case Studies." *Policy Studies Journal* 34(4): 699–722. doi:10.1111/j.1541-0072.2006.00198.x.

Wilson, W. J. 1980. *The Declining Significance of Race: Blacks and Changing American Institutions.* Chicago, IL: University of Chicago.

Woods, N. D. 2009. "Promoting Participation? An Examination of Rulemaking Notification and Access Procedures." *Public Administration Review* 69(3): 518–530. doi:10.1111/j.1540-6210.2009.01997.x.

Yang, K., and K. Callahan. 2007. "Citizen Involvement Efforts and Bureaucratic Responsiveness: Participatory Values, Stakeholder Pressures, and Administrative Practicality." *Public Administration Review* 67(2): 249–264. doi:10.1111/j.1540-6210.2007.00711.x.

Zvulun, J. 2010. *Political Participation and Engagement Aspect at the New Zealand Local Level.* Based on unpublished dissertation. University of Otago, NZ.

Index

Page references for figures are italicized.

About the Author

Ray C. Minor, PhD, is a senior associate at the Kettering Foundation. He has extensive executive and management experience in public, private, and nonprofit sectors. Minor's research interests include citizen participation and engagement, democracy, politics, public authorities and institutions, and nongovernmental organizations. He was Alabama director for UNCF/The College Fund. Minor served in the governor's cabinet in Alabama and held cabinet posts at a major nonprofit in New Jersey and two liberal arts colleges in Alabama and Texas. He was founding president and now chair emeritus of the David Mathews Center for Civic Life. Minor graduated from The University of Alabama with a bachelor of science in social welfare and a master's in higher education administration. Minor graduated from Walden University with a Doctor of Philosophy in public policy and administration. He was coeditor of *Beyond Politics as Usual: Paths for Engaging College Students in Politics* (2017). Minor was also author of *Reflections on President Barack Obama: The First President of Color of the United States* (2018) and *Donald J. Trump: The Tyrant in the White House* (2019). He is also author of *Straw Men, Paper Tigers and Puppets. The Philosophy of the Knowns and Unknowns* (2020).

www.ingramcontent.com/pod-product-compliance
Lightning Source LLC
LaVergne TN
LVHW011815200926
848484LV00005B/1206
* 9 7 8 1 7 9 3 6 1 7 4 8 4 *